IT <u>AIN'T</u> GONNA HAPPEN!™

A Return to Truth

By

A Friend of Medjugorje

IT <u>AIN'T</u> GONNA HAPPEN!™

A Return to Truth

By

A Friend of Medjugorje

Medjugorje

The Story in Brief

THE VILLAGE SEES THE LIGHT is the title of a story which "Reader's Digest" published in February 1986. It was the first major news on a mass public scale that told of the Virgin Mary visiting the tiny village of Medjugorje, Bosnia-Hercegovina. At that time this village was populated by 400 families.

It was June 24, 1981, the Feast of John the Baptist, the proclaimer of the coming Messiah. In the evening, around 5:00 p.m., the Virgin Mary appeared to two young people, Mirjana Dragičević* and Ivanka Ivanković*. Around 6:40 p.m. the same day, Mirjana and Ivanka, along with four more young people, Milka Pavlović*, the little sister of Marija, Ivan Ivanković, Vicka Ivanković*, and Ivan Dragičević saw the Virgin Mary. The next day, June 25, 1981, along with Mirjana, Ivanka, Vicka and Ivan Dragičević, Marija Pavlović* and Jakov Čolo also saw the Virgin Mary, bringing the total to six visionaries. Milka Pavlović* and Ivan Ivanković only saw Our Lady once, on that first day. These six have become known as and remain "the visionaries."

---

* Names at the time of the apparitions, the women are now married with last names changed.

These visionaries are not related to one another. Three of the six visionaries no longer see Our Lady on a daily basis. As of July 2010, the Virgin is still appearing everyday to the remaining three visionaries; that's well over 13,185 apparitions. The supernatural event has survived all efforts of the Communists to put a stop to it, many scientific studies, and even the condemnation by the local bishop; yet, the apparitions have survived, giving strong evidence that this is from God because nothing and no one has been able to stop it. For over twenty-nine years, the apparitions have proved themselves over and over and now credibility is so favorable around the world that the burden of proof that this is authentic has shifted from those who believe to the burden of proof that it is not happening by those opposed to it. Those against the apparitions are being crushed by the fruits of Medjugorje—millions and millions of conversions which are so powerful that they are changing and will continue to change the whole face of the earth.

See **mej.com** for more information.

---

* In the last ten to fifteen years, scores of Protestants are changing their view of Mary as a 'Catholic thing.' Many denominations are beginning to accept Her role as the Mother of Christ. Christ, being God, makes Mary, "Mother of God." Christ, our Brother, makes Mary our Mother.

Foreword

Minute upon minute, hour upon hour, day upon day reports are being given and discussions are taking place of what is happening with the economy. Predictions are made on both sides. Some are saying we have seen the worst of it, and things are changing around. Others are saying it will definitely get worse, but at least in the United States, we will not see the same kinds of social upheaval that other nations are suffering from—in other words, in our country, we'll be able to weather the storm. But Our Lady says: **"...Look at the signs of the times..."** May 2, 2009

Therefore, ask yourself the following questions:

- Why are people in great numbers today watching what they spend, taking fewer vacations, selling their boats and other luxury items, staying home for dinner instead of eating out?

- Why are so many people pulling their money and savings out of 'the investment markets' and putting it into something they believe is secure?

- Do you avoid thinking about what is coming in the future because you fear what could be coming?

- Is the falling economy one of the **"signs of the times"** that Our Lady has spoken about in Her messages?

- What sign did Our Lady give on June 24, 1981, that will help us understand why we are experiencing this economic upheaval?

- What if the economy doesn't spring back? What if it continues to fall?

- Is there any good coming from these bad economic times?

- Why have the gold and silver markets suddenly exploded over the past few years?

- Why is there such an interest in gardening right now, that even in the middle of city life, people are finding ways to grow their own food?

- Why is the size of your tomato plants and not the movement of the market the hot topic in the company break room?

- Why are people taking their homeowner's associations to court so they can raise chickens in their own backyards?

- Are you wishing you'd talked more to your grandparents about how they "used to do things?"

- When a snowstorm is forecasted, or a hurricane, we have all experienced how the grocery store shelves become emptied in just a few moments. Is the grocery store your cupboard? What would happen if a nation-wide/world-wide catastrophe hit, such as a total economic collapse? Do you believe those grocery store shelves will continue to be replenished with food in a breakdown of the economy?

- Are you living your life today as if the economy is going to get better soon, or are you seriously thinking and planning about how you and your family are going to survive if the economy completely crashes instead of turning around?

- When Our Lady said **"Be ready"** on April 2, 2010, what did She mean?

These questions are what this book is about. You don't

have to be a believer in the apparitions of Medjugorje to ponder the answers to the above questions. However, while so many are scratching their heads, wondering how we got ourselves into this situation, and wondering how we are going to get ourselves out of it, for those who are following Our Lady, the answers to the above questions are quite clear. She doesn't lead us to hopelessness, but rather She points the way to a better life. While many are just now entering the desert through these economic times, Our Lady is leading Her children who voluntarily entered the desert with Her years ago, out of the desert into the Promised Land. The Promised Land is not a place of ease and wealth, but rather a place where God provides for His children by way of their cooperating with Him for their provisions. Though this book speaks of spiritual matters in regards to the purpose of Our Lady's apparitions and our economic times, it also gives valuable information to the reader of what to do with your physical wealth to safeguard it in the case of economic collapse. There are many surprises within these pages that make <u>It Ain't Gonna Happen</u>_{TM} a delight to read, but its value lies in the fact that what is written is not being said anywhere else. As is his trademark, A Friend of Medjugorje doesn't pull any punches. While many want to look at the economic situation with rose-colored glasses, A

Friend of Medjugorje states quite plainly, without the white-wash that often accompanies economic reports, that we are headed towards very hard times. His confidence in stating this comes from what he, himself, has interiorly understood and has lived preceding and especially through Our Lady's apparitions and messages from Medjugorje for over a quarter of a century. A choice is to be made after reading this book: either you are going to put your head in the sand and continue to live your life as if everything will one day go back to 'normal', or you are going to change your life, and begin taking those steps that will eventually lead you out of the desert into the Promised Land, towards a new way of life Our Lady is showing us. But remember, whichever direction you decide on...the clock is ticking.

—The Publisher

ACKNOWLEDGEMENT

God alone deserves the credit for the publication of this book. It is from Him that the messages are allowed to be given through Our Lady to all of mankind. He alone deserves the praise and honor.

Table of Contents

Introduction

The following is an important and major writing. What is meant by 'major?' It means that contained in these pages are words that will educate you of things that before reading you were not aware. It means that you will be placed in a position of acting on these words, and it means you will receive guidance concerning what path to follow.

* * * * * * **A SPECIAL NOTE** * * * * * *

What you are about to read has been prayed about
for years. A great deal of discernment through Our
Lady's messages and the Holy Spirit has gone into
its contents. In our books and newsletters, we have
often recommended praying to the Holy Spirit for
understanding; however, the following should not even
be begun until it can be read slowly, in a contemplative
way, and without interruptions. As you read it, become
part of it. Find some quiet time or place such as in
front of the Blessed Sacrament or some other place
of solitude. If you are a Protestant, you may wish
to meditate and pray to the Holy Spirit for several
moments. If you are not sure of God, pray in your heart
to the God you do not know. He will manifest Himself
to you. Also, this book was not written to be read one
time only. It is to be read several times and each time
it is read, you will gain more understanding than the
previous reading. It would be wise to put off reading
this material until after much prayer. The Holy Spirit
will provide the necessary enlightenment and strength
to understand, and even to endure, the truth, which was
masterfully hidden from us but is now exposed to the
light by Our Lady through Her messages. Remember,
the following should only be read slowly, after prayer
to the Holy Spirit, and from the heart to grasp its full
meaning.

CHAPTER ONE

A "New" Efficacy

Have you ever sat down to read something and had no idea it would change the way you think about certain things, impel you to make decisions, and change your life? This is one of those writings. Therefore, it is important to pause, close your eyes and enter into a deep ardent prayer to the Holy Spirit that He will show and help you to understand all that is written, and not written, that Our Lady wants you to understand about your direction, your walk in life.

Our Lady said:

March 25, 1990

"...you must change the direction of your life..."

Why does Our Lady say change our direction? Our Lady tells us why:

January 25, 2009

"...I am with you for this long because you are on the wrong path..."

Do you think the whole world will change by Our Lady simply conveying a few times to pray the Rosary, go to church, be good, remember these things, good bye? The world is so grounded in its direction that Our Lady comes dressed in the color grey — a color which signifies servitude — as a servant who is ready to work, work hard, and work tirelessly to mop up the mess we have made of the world. Our Lady has encouraged us, witnessed to us, reprimanded us, and pushed us, all through love, to change the direction of our lives. She tells us, **"Thank you for responding to my call,"** though all the while we do not deserve a thank you for our efforts, because we continually fall short of Her desires. Yet, in thanking us for our response, She does so with the hope of it raising our impulse to respond, thereby inciting us to live more fully Her 'Words from Heaven.' Our Lady's tools to change us are many because, for centuries, She has been with us, appearing in apparitions throughout the centuries. She gave us the Rosary—1213, the Brown Scapular—1251, the Miraculous Image on the Tilma in Guadalupe, Mexico—1531, the Miraculous Medal at Rue du Bac, in Paris, France—1830, springs for healing and inciting faith in Lourdes, France—1858, the miracle of the sun in Fatima, Portugal—1917, among many other tools. And now, Our Lady comes to Medjugorje* - 1981, and made it a miraculous village, a surreal spiritual happening, a tool through which She <u>will</u> change the direction of the world. Our Lady said May, 1984:

"Throughout the centuries, I have given myself completely to you..."

Our Lady has accumulated a lot of spiritual tools throughout the centuries that were the cause of countless millions of conversions. But some may respond, Medjugorje is the 'now' apparition. What is in the past is past. So, by Our Lady coming, do these spiritual tools She has given in the past, not have the same grace attached to them? It may seem so, except for the Rosary. The Rosary was first used in 1213 against the King of Aragon and his army of over 40,000 soldiers who had arrived in Muret, France, to attack the Catholic chieftain and his outnumbered army of 800 soldiers.[1] Through the Rosary, the small force, numbering 800, defeated 40,000! We all realize, with the Medjugorje apparitions, the Rosary is not only just as powerful of a tool, but even more so than when introduced. This was even confirmed December 26, 1957, when the visionary of Fatima, Sr. Lucia, told Fr. Augustin Fuentes:

---

* Find more information on Medjugorje.com

*"Look father, the Most Holy Virgin, in these last times in which we live, has given a **new efficacy** to the recitation of the Rosary. She has given this **efficacy to such an extent** that there is no problem, no matter how difficult it is, whether temporal or above all spiritual, in the personal life of each one of us, of our family, of the families of the world, or of the religious communities, or even of the life of peoples and nations, that cannot be solved by the Rosary. There is no problem I tell you, no matter how difficult it is, that we cannot resolve by the prayer of the Holy Rosary."[2]*

Efficacy means: *the power to produce an effect.*

If you balk at Sr. Lucia's words, notice how she addresses the priest, "Look Father!" — who also must have had a hard time with Lucia's words that with the Rosary there is nothing that cannot be resolved.

Sr. Lucia said, "in these last times." Our Lady gives a **'new'** efficacy in a quantitative way, to an extent that the world has never before known in its use and power of the Rosary. When one prays the Rosary for any or every thing, for any licit condition or intention, there is nothing on the face of the earth — again, there is nothing — that cannot be resolved!!

But is that the case for other spiritual tools of conversion and miracles of the past? Do they still hold the
grace as when they were first released? For instance, in
Guadalupe, Mexico, Juan Diego's Tilma, with the image
placed upon it by Our Lady, instantly converted millions
as they looked upon it in 1531. Aside from the Rosary,
do these other external signs, such as the Tilma, still carry
the grace to the degree of their initial origin? Most would
have to answer no, they do not. Is it that the grace attached to them no longer produces the same conversions
because we no longer believe with an enthusiastic faith?
Has the lack of miracles resulted from our becoming ac-
customed to these signs, the Tilma, Miraculous Medal, etc.,
and, thereby, through a spiritual apathy, we do not even
contemplate them anymore, let alone have an expectation
that they will still produce miracles, except rarely?

Regardless of whether these signs have the same
power as they had in the past, one thing is certain. We do
know Medjugorje's grace is in this present moment, in
this immediate age and through Medjugorje, conversions
are abounding into the millions, just as these other spiritual tools of the past caused conversions into the millions
when they were in the immediate age. However, through
Our Lady encountering us through the centuries, we are
able to recognize today these past apparitions as pieces of

a puzzle given to us through the centuries. Once put together, these pieces give the **'image'** of the whole puzzle.
That image is a place between two mountains, framed in
a Holy Trinity triangle of Apparition Mountain, Cross
Mountain, and the Church — a triangle image of salvation; Apparition Mountain representing Our Lady, Cross
Mountain representing Jesus Christ and the sign of our
salvation, and St. James Church representing the Church.
Unlike Our Lady's image given to Juan Diego, which
only gives a piece of the puzzle, as do Lourdes, Fatima,
etc., Medjugorje brings together the full puzzle's image,
the complete picture. *Medjugorje* is not only for the immediate age, but for all ages to come, the place of the fulfillment of all Her apparitions forever! Our Lady says:

May 2, 1982

"...I will not appear any more on this earth."

Medjugorje is the site of the last apparitions on earth
in which visionaries are able to see Our Lady, talk to Her,
and touch Her. Our Lady said these apparitions will fully
complete the need of why She has come throughout history in apparitions to the earth. There will never again be
the type of apparitions such as the visionaries of Lourdes,
Fatima, and Medjugorje experienced because there will
no longer be a need. This is why Medjugorje is the fulfillment of all Marian apparitions.

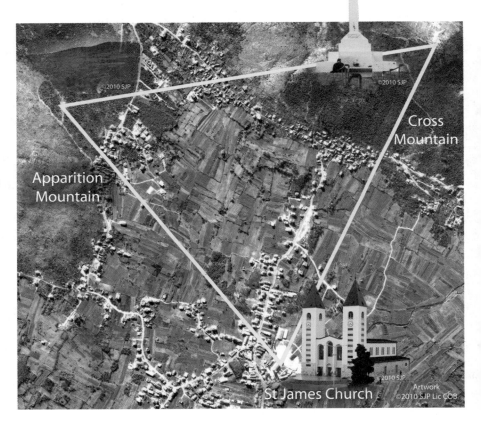

The word 'Medjugorje' means "between the mountains." Our Lady first appeared below the summit of Mt. Podbrdo, which became known as Apparition Mountain. The date was June 24, 1981. On 6/24 She came holding something in Her arms, what the children first believed was a little lamb. They were not entirely wrong as She was holding Her infant Son, Jesus, The Lamb of God. 6/24 was the feast day of St. John the Baptist, who was the herald of the Messiah, the forerunner chosen by God to prepare the way of the Lord. The topography of Medjugorje has within it a Biblical and mystical blueprint in which the history of salvation is readily seen in the three most prominent points recognized within the village: Apparition Mountain, Cross Mountain and St. James Church form a triangle, a Holy Trinity, that while speaking of the past, also points to the future. The triangle is nearly perfect when tilted in which Apparition Mountain and the Church make up the base, for both point to the summit of our salvation, 'the Cross.' Our Lady does not only come as the modern day John the Baptist, though the date 6/24, John the Baptist's feast-day, is significantly symbolic. Our Lady is coming, as She preceded Her Son 2,000 years ago, except this time to call the world <u>back</u> to Her Son in preparation for His glorious second coming.

Our Lady said on March 18, 1996, "**...My eyes and my heart will be here, even when I will no longer appear...**" There will be a strong spirit of Our Lady present in the world when these apparitions end, a stronger spiritual presence than what was known and felt before Her Medjugorje Apparitions. Our Lady will never again appear on earth like She does to the Medjugorje visionaries. This is not to say She will not someday come to a pious person in a much lesser form, such as has happened many times in interior locutions,* for example, or in our hearts. However, Our Lady, as She told us in the above March 18, 1996, message, will be with us in a new way, a new capacity, with a strong attentive presence upon the earth. It, however, is certain that Our Lady did say that these apparitions, in which a visionary can see Her, talk to Her, and touch Her, never again will be seen on earth. Being with the Holy Virgin Mary in the fullness of reality of Her resurrected, glorified body, as in Medjugorje, will have come and gone, never to return anywhere upon the earth. 'Woe' to those who ignore the opportunity Medjugorje affords them today, knowing when this moment passes, there will no longer be the fullness of the Holy Virgin Mary's presence experienced by man on earth.

---

* Interiorly and spiritually hearing the voice of Our Lady in one's heart while in prayer; not a physical manifestation.

CHAPTER TWO

Setting the Stage

All that was written in the previous chapter is stated for the **"Setting of the Stage"** for a very significant message Our Lady gave to Medjugorje visionary, Marija. This message was overlooked by many of us because it was given years ago during one of the prayer group meetings. It has gone mostly unnoticed until now. Before you read this special message, it is important to understand the following. Being called to spread Our Lady's messages through Medjugorje, we, at Caritas, have never overly concerned ourselves with past apparitions. When the Messiah came, those who had followed John the Baptist, after recognizing the Messiah, were called to leave John and to follow Jesus. They went to the immediate. In the same way, we promote the immediate of Medjugorje. Our Lady says:

January 25, 1997

"...This time is my time..."

All the past apparitions of the Holy Virgin Mary in 1213, 1251, 1531, etc., are the steps leading up to the throne over the world in which its Queen in **this, Her time,** will be recognized and acknowledged by all the earth, the summit of all apparitions — Medjugorje! It doesn't matter if you are Protestant, a non-church Christian, Muslim, etc., you will accept Her. Eyes of all will be opened to Her Throne as the Queen of Peace, next to Jesus' Throne as the King of Peace. Even hordes of non-believers will turn to Her and love Her. The only exceptions of those who will not will be those who deliberately hate and reject God while on earth. These poor souls already live hell in this life and will simply continue a much more grave hell into the next life. But it is Our Lady who has come to the earth to do everything in Her power to reach all souls. Those familiar with Medjugorje have heard miracle after miracle that are associated with Our Lady in the apparitions of Medjugorje. It is also clear to those who know Medjugorje, that these miracles, millions upon millions of them, little ones and big ones, surpass any specific era of the Church in regards to their numbers.

This understood, we, at Caritas, only promote what is directly related to the messages of Medjugorje. We believe very strongly in the Scapular devotion and all of us in community wear this beautiful gift. However, it is not our charism to spend our efforts in promoting the Scapular or other devotions. We leave this to others whose charism calls them to such. But one may respond, *"Caritas does promote other things, for example, the Poem of the Man-God. That is not Medjugorje."* Caritas promotes what is directly tied to Our Lady's messages, including that which Our Lady mandates through Her messages of Medjugorje. This is why Caritas promotes Maria Valtorta's five volumes of The Poem of the Man-God. Our Lady was questioned by one of the six Medjugorje visionaries, Marija, on behalf of a seminarian, if these books could be read.

1982–1983

> Marija went before Our Lady on behalf of a seminarian and asked the question: *"Was it okay to read the book The Poem of the Man-God?"* Marija relayed that Our Lady not only affirmed reading them was okay, but that She said:
>
> **"One must read them."**

As a result of the discovery of this message, and Marija verifying the message in the middle to end of the 1980s, Caritas immediately began promoting the five volumes because Our Lady said, **"One must read them."**

Caritas quickly became the main promoter of these works across the United States, introducing thousands of people to these wonderful writings which are a great help in understanding and comprehending Our Lady's messages. Hence, Our Lady said, **"One must read them."** A huge wave of persecution came against Caritas because of our effort. But an edict that came through Cardinal Ratzinger, now Pope Benedict XVI, with the blessing of Pope John Paul II directly to Caritas, cleared the way worldwide for all to read these volumes. However, what is important is Our Lady tied the <u>The Poem of the Man-God</u> volumes to Medjugorje as part of Her messages.

The point being made by this example is that being followers of Our Lady's apparitions in Medjugorje, we recognize the importance of other apparition sites that helped to create devotion and a following for Our Lady, such as Fatima and Lourdes, but at the same time, Medjugorje is happening in our time. Medjugorje offers a 'live' grace, meaning that nothing from the past has the same potency of grace that Medjugorje is offering man today. However, if through Our Lady's messages in Medjugorje She makes known something that has attached to it special graces for our time, even if it has come through a past apparition in a different time of history, we accept and embrace that gift and firmly establish it into our lives.

CHAPTER THREE

Do You Know Someone
Who Needs Conversion?
Releasing The Greatness of The Message

On July 4, 1982, visionaries Ivan and Marija, together with a group of their friends, started a prayer group at the request of Our Lady. They would meet together on Apparition or Cross Mountain, pray and sing together, and Our Lady would appear to Ivan and Marija, often times giving a message or making a request for prayer for a special intention. When Marija married and began having children, she was no longer able to consistently go to the prayer group, but Ivan continued, and the prayer group became known as Ivan's prayer group as it is still called today.

Now that we've set the stage for the very significant message, you will read why Caritas will promote what Our Lady asks for in this special message She gave to Marija during one of the prayer group meetings. It is a call to renew, to evangelize and to reinvigorate devotion to one of Her past spiritual tools that was the impetus of millions of conversions and many other divine graces. A call from the past in regards to utilizing a 'spiritual tool' is now a call of today from Our Lady, Queen of Peace of Medjugorje, to activate Her children with a renewed spirit, with the knowledge of Her words as She expressed a desire of Hers to spread this devotion. The message is one of simplicity, but one that should not be discounted as of little significance because Our Lady's messages contain **'greatness'** that few, very few, really and truly comprehend. One cannot comprehend these simple messages without serious and long term daily prayer to *unlock* the greatness of these messages. Before you read this special, significant message to Marija, first read another message Our Lady gave to help you understand in what context Our Lady Herself holds Her words. Our Lady said on October 25, 1988:

> **"...my call that you live the messages which I am giving you is a daily one...pray that you may comprehend the <u>greatness</u> of this message which I am giving you..."**

Keep these words in mind as you read the following message so you may, as Our Lady says, "...**comprehend the greatness...**" Read in prayer and in depth to realize the following message Our Lady wishes for Her children to activate and initiate into their lives and evangelization efforts. The following is the description and message:

The following happened on **Monday, November 27, 1989.** The prayer group meeting was at the Blue Cross, at the base of Apparition Mountain in Medjugorje at 10:00 P.M.

This message was given to Marija, who was standing in for Ivan. Our Lady came joyful and She said:

"These days, I want you to pray in a special way for the salvation of souls. Today is the feast day of the Miraculous Medal, and I want that you pray, in a special way, for the salvation of those people who are carrying this Miraculous Medal. I want you to spread the devotion and the carrying of this medal, so that more souls may be saved, and that you pray in a special way."

Without serious prayer, one may think this message of Our Lady is insignificant, as many people think of Our Lady's messages, not comprehending them. But do you see the **'greatness'** of the message? It is not only to be viewed with greatness as Our Lady asks us to **comprehend** them, but eleven months before the above Miraculous Medal message, Our Lady also said the living of Her messages is a life of **profoundness**. Our Lady said on December 4, 1988:

"I invite you to live the *profoundness* of the messages that I give."

To pray and **comprehend** the Miraculous Medal message of Medjugorje, with the **greatness** and the **profoundness** of carrying out the messages in one's life, start by just reading what Our Lady is offering Her children in giving us this direction. Our Lady began the message with **'These days.'** This is not 1830, when St. Catherine is seeing and talking to Our Lady, rather it is 1989 when Medjugorje visionary Marija is seeing and talking to Our Lady. Our Lady spoke to both of them — St. Catherine to inaugurate the medal's use and Marija to re-inaugurate its use. By Marija telling us of the 'Miraculous Medal,' this can only mean that Our Lady will still, today, save souls through it, even to a greater degree. So, it is important that we spread it!

Our Lady says the following things in Her Miraculous Medal message of 1989 that reveal the greatness of Her messages:

1. **"These days,"**
   from 1989 when the message was given, to these current times of Her Medjugorje apparitions.

2. **"I want"**
   is said three times to emphasize this **"want."** Who wants? It is the Blessed Virgin Mother.

3. **"Feast day of the Miraculous Medal"**
    brings significance to a day that most today hard-
    ly give credence to because, even though souls
    still wear the medal, it is generally considered by
    most a thing of the past in regard to miracles.

4. **"Pray in a special way"**
    is said three times to emphasize the serious re-
    quest for this, in current times, and to help us to
    comprehend that we are not to pray in our nor-
    mal way. Rather, we must pray in a 'special' way,
    in the spirit of the messages which formed a 'new
    special way of life.'

5. **"Salvation of souls," "salvation of those people",
    "more souls may be saved"** —
    three times Our Lady refers to the purpose of
    this message which is to increase the number of
    souls that can be saved through Her Miraculous
    Medal.

6. **"Those people who are carrying this Miraculous
    Medal."**
    Our Lady signifies that 'those people,' who are
    carrying the medal are marked with a hope for
    Her to convert them and dispense to them the
    grace of salvation. Our Lady does not originate

the grace, only God can, but He (God) gives them to Her to dispense.

7. **"I want 'you' to spread the devotion."**
   'You' are commissioned by the Queen of Peace of Medjugorje to spread 'the' devotion.

8. **"I want 'you' to spread...the carrying of this medal."**
   'You' are commissioned to encourage and spread the physical carrying of this medal.

9. **"I want...that 'you' pray in a special way."**
   'You' are to:

   * Pray for the salvation of souls.

   * Pray for those carrying the medal.

   * Pray to spread the 'devotion' and the carrying of the medal.

Three distinct and different requests Our Lady makes of you:

   * To pray for the salvation of souls marked by the medal.

   * To encourage the carrying of the medal.

   * To spread devotion to the Miraculous Medal.

CHAPTER FOUR

The Story in Brief of St. Catherine Laboure and the Miraculous Medal

In the year 1830, there lived a young novice, Sr. Catherine Laboure, who had just entered the Daughters of Charity. She was placed in the Mother house in Paris, located on Rue du Bac. Catherine had gone to bed on July 18, 1830, but at half past eleven she was awoken by a brilliant light. She heard a child's voice say, "Sister Laboure, come to the Chapel; the Blessed Mother wishes to speak to you." The voice belonged to a small child who Catherine came to believe was her guardian angel. He led her to the Chapel and upon hearing the rustling of a silk dress, she looked up and beheld the Blessed Virgin Mary sitting in a chair near the altar. Catherine knelt down beside Her, placing her folded hands upon Our Lady's lap. The Blessed Mother began to speak to Catherine informing her that God had chosen her for a special mission. The Virgin became sad when She began to reveal to Catherine that very difficult times were coming for the Church and that there would be much persecution and bloodshed. In tears, Our Lady said that the Cross of Her Son would be treated with contempt.

After this apparition, Our Lady appeared to Catherine on two more occasions. In the apparition of November 27, 1830, Our Lady appeared holding a golden ball. She said this ball represented the entire world, and in particular, France. Then the apparition changed and Catherine was shown a medal, both the front and backside and was told by Our Lady to have this medal struck and spread. Though it took two years to convince her confessor, it was finally produced and distributed. Immediately people began to experience miracles that they associated with the medal which led to it being called the 'Miraculous Medal'. For certain, this apparition to St. Catherine, the past apparitions in history leading up to this, and the medal itself opened up a floodgate of graces, inaugurating the coming of the Marian era. Medjugorje has ushered in this Marian era with Our Lady appearing daily for almost 30 years in this our time. This era, with Our Lady's apparitions in Medjugorje, is the fulfillment of all Her apparitions throughout history.

CHAPTER FIVE

Astounding True Story

Millions of miracles occurred as a result of St. Catherine's superior finally allowing the Miraculous Medal to be struck as Our Lady had requested. One famous conversion took place on January 20, 1842, when a man, after being encouraged to wear this medal, saw Our Lady. He was not a Christian, but a Jew! He, Alphonse Ratisbonne, became a priest, and it sparked such enthusiasm for the medal that the Vatican looked into this case, Ratisbonne's apparition, and the Miraculous Medal. But that was January 20, 1842.[3] What about now? Are there any profound graces linked to the Miraculous Medal in our modern times to encourage us? Does the Miraculous Medal still carry the same graces of conversion as when it was released in 1832? Yes, there is a story and the date, not by accident, coincides with the January 20 conversion of the Jewish man of 1842. This later miracle took place in the year 1943. The following story tells of this miracle, right about 100 years to the day of this significant date, January 20, in regard to the life of Claude Newman.

The Story of Claude Newman

Claude Newman was a young negro man, a man of odd jobs, living in Mississippi when in the early 1940s, he became involved in incredible events in the last four to five months of his life.

He was born on December 1, 1923 in Stuttgart, Arkansas. When Claude was five years old, his father separated from his mother and took Claude and his older brother to Bovina, Mississippi, located east of Vicksburg, where Ellen Newman, Claude's grandmother, lived. From this point on, Claude Newman and his brother were raised by their grandmother. When Claude was in his teenage years, his grandmother married Sid Cook, a 60-year old black man who had been born and raised on U.G. Flowers Plantation in Bovina, Mississippi, known as Ceres Plantation. Sid remained as a tenant farmer on the plantation basically his entire life, although Ellen separated from Sid after three years of marriage and no longer lived in the same house.

On December 19, 1942, 19-year-old Claude, aware Sid had just been paid and had money, went to Sid's home and lay in wait for him. With indifference and in cold-hearted blood, he shot Sid with a shotgun after Sid came into the house. Claude then went through his pockets, taking a small purse and some loose bills totaling at least $141.00. Taking Sid's money, Claude then fled to his mother's home in Little Rock, Arkansas, arriving the next day. His mother, Floretta, had not seen her son since he was five-years-old. She was then remarried to a man by the name of Rogers who found work for Claude. Before going to work, Claude changed his name to Ralph.

A few weeks went by before the F.B.I. caught up with Claude and returned him to Vicksburg. He went to trial, was convicted of murder and sentenced to die by means of the electric chair. Though Claude's attorney tried to object to Claude's confession, stating it was coerced, the court rejected this argument, as Claude's confession had been attended by a sheriff, the District Attorney, a stenographer, and a black minister. After witnessing the confession, they all re-read the confession to make sure nothing was added. The four signed the confession with Claude initializing each page as it was re-read to him to make sure he also agreed with its accuracy. In the trial, all four of them testified that there was no duress in any way at all.[4]

Fr. Robert O'Leary, SVD (1911–1984) became involved with Claude while he (Claude) was on death row. What follows is taken from a transcript in which he relayed from his personal involvement the facts concerning Claude Newman's final months before the date was set for his execution, **January 20, 1944**. January 20 was the day of the conversion of the Jewish man Alphonse Ratisbonne about 100 years before.

One morning in the fall of 1943, after my morning Mass, I was notified by the pastor that there was a call for me at the county jail. There was a prisoner there, Claude Newman, who was screaming that he had to have a Catholic priest and he wanted to see one immediately. I hesitated to go because I had classes but my pastor told me that I had to go, so I went.

While on my way, I was totally unconscious of the fact that I had become violently angry. I was like a demon from the lower regions the way I was behaving.

I got to the jail and said, *"Where is that one who wants me?"*

When I was brought up to him, he said to me, *"Are you a Catholic priest?"* At that moment, all the anger and all the violence in me left me.

The night before, Claude said that he and four other men were talking in the cell block, and when they ran out of conversation, Claude saw a medal on a string around another prisoner's neck. He asked what it was and the Catholic boy told him that it was a medal. He said, *"What is a medal?"* And the Catholic boy could not explain what the medal was or its purpose. In anger, the Catholic boy snatched the medal from off his own neck and threw it on the floor at Claude's feet with a curse, telling him to take the so-and-so thing.

Claude called a prison trustee and got a piece of string and tied it around his own neck. To him it was only a bobble, a trinket. But during the night, sleeping on top of his cot, he was awakened with a touch on his wrist. And there stood, as he told me, the most beautiful woman that God ever created. He was scared at first. She calmed him and then She said to him, **"If you would like Me to be your Mother and you would like to be My child, send for a priest of the Catholic Church."** And with that She disappeared.

If Claude had been shaken before, he was now terrified. He screamed, *"A haunt!"* meaning *'a ghost!' 'a ghost!'* and fled to the cell of one of the other prisoners. All night long he kept screaming he wanted a priest, he wanted a priest.

While Claude told me all this, I listened to him but I didn't believe him. The other prisoners told me that everything was true, though they could not have known anything about the vision except for what Claude told them. But it shook them enough that after I talked to them awhile, they wanted Catholic instruction to become Catholic. So I promised to come back and bring it to them.

On my way downstairs I stopped off to see the jailer whom I had scandalized on my way up, not really knowing at all that I had scandalized him. I asked him how his family was. And he said, *"Oh! You're calm and rational? You're not as crazy as you were coming upstairs."* He said, *"And boy, Father, you know words I didn't think anybody knew."* I went home very humiliated and very much ashamed of myself. I told Fr. Francis, my pastor, what had happened. Claude Newman had also told me that the Blessed Mother said this is exactly how I would come. That the devil would try to stop me in order to scandalize and drive Claude away!

The next day I went back with the Catechisms. And then I found that Claude Newman could not read or write a word. The only time he could tell if a book was upright was if there was a picture in it. He had never been one single day in a classroom in his life. And as his ignorance of human knowledge was so deep, his ignorance of religion was even deeper. He knew nothing at all about religion. He did not know who Jesus was, he did not know anything except that there was a God. Period. We began the instruction and the prisoners helped Claude and after a few days of giving instructions, two religious sisters who were teachers in our school, asked if they could come to the jail. They wanted to see Claude. They also wanted to see the women in the jail. Sheriff Williamson gave permission, and so the sisters began going to the jail and giving instructions to the women, while I ran upstairs and gave instructions to the men.

Several weeks passed and it came time where I was going to begin instructions on the Sacrament of Penance. Just before I was going to start, the two sisters finished their classes downstairs and got permission to go upstairs. The trustee put two chairs outside the cell block for them and one sat on each side of me.

And I said to them, *"Boys, we're going to start talking about the Sacrament of Confession, of Penance."* And Claude said to me, *"Oh, I know that! She told me that when we go to Confession, we are kneeling down, not before a priest, but we're kneeling down by the Cross of Her Son. And that when we are truly sorry for our sins and we confess our sins, the blood He shed flows down over us and washes us free from our sins."*

Well, the sisters and I sat there with our mouths wide open, and Claude took it that we were angry. He said to me, *"Oh don't be angry! Don't be angry. I didn't mean to blurt it out."* I said, *"I'm not angry. I'm just amazed. You have seen Her again?"* He said, *"Come around the cell block away from the others."* And so I did. And he said to me, *"She told me that if you doubted me or showed hesitancy I was to remind you, that laying in a ditch in Holland in 1940 you made a vow to Her which She's still waiting for you to keep."* And he told me exactly what the vow was. Needless to say I was converted.

We went back and Claude kept telling the other fellas, *"You should not be afraid to go to Confession. You're really telling God your sins, not this priest or any other priest. We're telling God our sins."* He said, *"You know, She said something like a telephone — we talk through the priest to God, and God talks back to us through the priest."*

So, about a week later, we were going to speak about the Blessed Sacrament. And Claude said, *"Well, you won't get angry with me will you?"* I said, *"No."* And the sisters were there too. Claude said, *"Well, Our Lady told me in Communion I will only see what looks like a piece of bread. But She told me that that is really and truly Her*

Son, and that He will be with me just for a few moments as He was with Her before He was born in Bethlehem. She said that I should spend my time like She did in all Her time with Him, by loving Him, adoring Him, thanking Him, praising Him and asking Him for the blessings. I shouldn't be bothered about anybody else or anything else. And I should spend my two or three minutes with Him." I said, *"Well, Claude there's nothing I can add to that."* I said, *"It's perfect."*

So, time went on. We finished the instructions and the day came when Claude was to be executed, **January 20**, 1944. Claude was to be executed at five minutes after twelve midnight. The Sheriff asked him, *"Claude, you have the privilege of a last request. What do you want?"* He said, *"Well, Sheriff,"* he said, *"You're all shook up. The jailer is all shook up, but"* he said, *"you don't understand. I'm not going to die. Just this body. I am going to be with Her. So, can I have a party?"*

And the Sheriff said, *"Well what do you mean by a party?"* Claude said, *"Well, will you give Father permission to bring in some cakes and some ice cream and would you allow the prisoners on the second floor to be all turned loose into the main center of the room so that we can all be together and have a party?"* And the Sheriff said, *"Yeah, but somebody might attack Father."* He said, *"Oh no. No-*

body will attack him. Will you fellas?" Everybody said
no.

So I went down the street to a Mrs. Morrissey who
was one of the richest ladies in town. And she sent up
ten gallons of ice cream and five or six large cakes. That
night at seven o'clock in the evening we had our party,
and after the party, because Claude had requested it, I
brought prayer books from the church and we said the
Stations of the Cross and we had a Holy Hour without the Blessed Sacrament being present. Then I put
the men back in their cells and the door to the lower
floor was opened and I was able to go down. I went to
the church and came back with the Blessed Sacrament
and Claude knelt on one side of the bars and I on the
other and we prayed together. Fifteen minutes before
the execution was to take place, the Sheriff came running up the stairs and he said, *"Reprieve! Reprieve! The
Governor has given a two week reprieve. Claude, we're
still trying to save you."*

Claude, up to this time, did not know that Sheriff
Williamson and Mr. Bill Ballard, the District Attorney, both white, were trying to save his life. Claude
broke down. We thought it was a reaction from the
fact that he was not going to die. And he said, *"Oh you
men don't know. And Father you don't know. If you ever*

looked into Her face and looked into Her eyes you wouldn't want to live another day. What have I done wrong in these past weeks that God would take and refuse me my going home?"

Claude sobbed absolutely like a broken-hearted person. The sheriff went away, and I stayed there. And I said to him, *"Claude, it's after midnight. Let me give you Communion."* He received Communion, quieted down, and then he said to me, *"Why? Why must I still remain here for two weeks?"*

And without any thought I said to him, *"Well Claude, now you know that white prisoner, James Hughes over there who hates you so much? Of all the other people up here, he hates you more than he hates any other person.* Maybe Our Blessed Mother wants you to offer this denial of being with Her for his conversion."* And he said, *"What would that be?"* And I said, *"Well, why don't you take and offer to God every moment you're still separated from Her for him, that he would not be separated from God for all eternity."*

He quieted down. I left my crucifix with him and I went home. I came back later that day in the afternoon. Claude was very quiet and calm. He gave me

---

* This was not a racial hatred. Hughes was on good terms with some of his black neighbors, according to court records..

back my crucifix and he said, *"Yes,"* he added, *"I'm going to pray for him. But,"* he said, *"I have news for you."*

I said, *"What?"*

He said, *"That man, Hughes, hated me before, but oh Father, how he hates me now."*

I said, *"Well, that's a good sign, that's a good sign."*

Two weeks passed and Claude went to his death. I've never seen anybody go to death as joyfully and as happy. Even the official witnesses and the newspaper reporters were amazed. They said they couldn't understand how anybody could go and sit in the electric chair, actually beaming with happiness.

And his last words to me were, *"Father, I will remember you. And whenever you have a request ask me and I will ask Her."*

Two months later, the white man was to be executed. Let me fill you in on James Hughes. Hughes had left his wife. He had two sons and two daughters. He took the children with him, they were teenagers, and he was hiding out in Warren County. When his wife discovered where he was, trying to get the girls back, she had deputies sent out to get them. This man killed a deputy. Hughes was taken in and arrested. Hughes was the filthiest, most immoral person I've ever come across. His hatred for God, his hatred for everything spiritual defies description.

Well, the time came for his execution. Dr. Podesta, who was the county doctor, pleaded with him to at least kneel down and say the Our Father before the sheriff would come for him.

He spit in the doctor's face.

They manacled him, dragged him down to the chair and in the chair the sheriff said to him, *"If you have something to say, say it now."* And he started to blaspheme.

All of a sudden he stopped and he looked up towards the corner and his face was one of absolute horror. Hughes let out a scream and then said, *"Oh, Sheriff, get me a priest."*

I happened to be in the room because the law required a clergyman. I was hiding behind two deputies and a newspaper reporter because this man said he would curse God if he saw a clergyman at all. Now he was calling for a priest.

One of the deputies turned around and said, *"Father, he's calling for a priest."*

I stepped out and said, *"Here I am."*

He said, *"Father, hear my confession. I'm a Catholic."* He had been raised in a Catholic home until he was 18. And then because of his immorality and his refusal to convert and behave himself, he was refused absolution by a priest, justifiably so, and he left the Church with hatred. The sheriff cleaned the room out and I heard his confession. I stood by the side of the chair. He confessed all of his sins and I gave him absolution. I signaled for the sheriff and the others to come back.

When they came back, Sheriff Williamson, devout Episcopalian that he was said, *"Father, what changed that guy's mind?"*

I said, *"I don't know. I didn't ask him."*

He said, *"Well, I'll never sleep if I don't."* He said, *"Son, what changed your mind?"*

And Hughes said, *"Well, Sheriff, you remember that black man that I hated so much?"*

The Sheriff said, *"Yes."*

Hughes said, *"Well, he's standing still over there in that corner. And behind him, with one hand on each shoulder is the Blessed Mother. And Claude said to me, 'I offered my death in union with Christ's on the cross for your salva-*

tion. She has obtained for you this gift. See your place in hell if you don't repent.'" He then saw himself in Hell. And that was when he screamed.

The execution took place. The Sheriff said to me, *"I wonder, what do you mean by 'I offer my death with Christ on the cross?'"*

I said, *"Sheriff, there were only two people who knew this: Claude Newman and myself. Just before Claude's execution, he looked at me and said: "The Blessed Mother wants me to offer my death in union with Her Son. Will you help me say the right words?"* [5]

This validated what Father had already suggested to Claude, that he should offer up his death for Hughes' salvation when he (Claude) found out he had a reprieve for two more weeks.

And I said, *"Kneeling side by side each other by the bars, we made that offering of his life and his death in union with Christ on the cross for the salvation of James Hughes."*

I said, *"Claude and Mary came to tell that man that he was saved. We must never underestimate the power of Mary."* [6]

* * * * * * * * * *

What was discovered during the research of this story was that there was yet a third documented con-

version among the convicted murderers, found in a
newspaper report. Mildred James, "a young negro
woman" was also sentenced to death by electrocution.
She had murdered an *"aged spinster who lived alone in
a rambling old home near the city limits"*[7] of Vicksburg.
Mildred went to her death ten minutes before James
Hughes on the same day, in the same electric chair. Eye
witnesses said that Mildred walked calmly to the chair
without assistance, and just before the eye guards were
placed over her eyes, she looked at the Catholic priest,
*"which faith she had embraced several weeks before, and
faintly smiled."*[8] Mildred was the first woman ever to
be executed in the State of Mississippi.[9] Recalling in
Fr. O'Leary's testimony that two religious sisters, after
hearing about Claude Newman, became interested in
sharing the Catholic faith with the women prisoners, we
can presume that Mildred was the fruit from those visits—which also can then be accredited to Claude Newman's conversion through the Miraculous Medal!

This is the power of Our Lady's Miraculous Medal, and
Our Lady in our time is making a fresh direct request to
spread the medal.

What was the secret Our Lady told Claude, that when
he revealed it to the priest, convinced Father O'Leary
beyond any doubt he had seen Our Lady?

The promise Fr. O'Leary made to Our Lady in 1940 from a ditch in Holland, the proof Claude gave the priest that Our Lady really was appearing to him, was this: that when he could, he would build a church in honor of **Our Lady's Immaculate Conception**. He had not fulfilled this promise to Our Lady which was known to no one except himself and Our Lady. Needless to say, after Claude's revelation from Our Lady of this secret promise, he knew without a doubt that Claude talked to Our Lady. Father later built the church in 1947 in Clarksdale, Mississippi, where he had been transferred. The Bishop of Natchez contributed $5,000 from the Archbishop Cushing of Boston. The church is still there today.[10]

The fact that Fr. O'Leary had promised Our Lady to build a church in Her honor and to name it the Immaculate Conception Church was also an amazing 'coincidence' as the words on the Miraculous Medal state: *"O Mary, conceived without sin, pray for us who have recourse to Thee."* These words were prophetic in that they were given in 1830, but the Church did not officially define the Immaculate Conception as Dogma until later, on December 8, 1854. On March 25, 1858, four years after the Dogma had been declared, Our Lady, appearing to St. Bernadette in Lourdes, gave Her title, saying to Bernadette, "I am the **Immaculate Conception**."

For Fr. O'Leary, then, to be inspired to want to build a church under the name of the **"Immaculate Conception"** 100 years after Our Lady's involvement with St. Catherine and St. Bernadette, and before he became involved with Claude Newman could only have happened through the inspiration of the Holy Spirit.

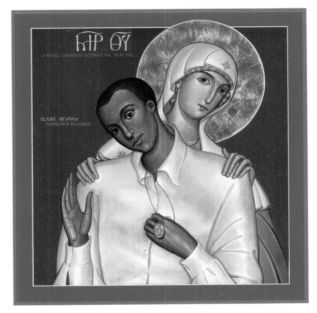

Br. Claude Lane from Mount Angel Abbey became interested in Claude New-man's story when he happened upon it in 2002. Br. Claude, being moved by the incredible story of Claude's conversion, used the gift of his art to tell Claude's story in an icon which he named "Mary, the Teacher." It depicts what con-demned prisoner Hughes saw after being strapped to the electric chair.

A prisoner on death row, awaiting his execution date, resulted in this church in Clarksdale, Mississippi, being built. A most remarkable story concerning a priest and convicted felons and their involvement with the origins of The Immaculate Conception Catholic Church.

The Warren County Jail is where Claude Newman was contained after being arrested and subsequently, convicted of murdering Sid Cook. After being sentenced to death by electrocution, he had only a few months to live.

Though the jail has been added onto and renovated over the years, the original building is still in existence. According to the article in the *Vicksburg Evening Post*, Claude *"...walked from his cell on the second floor of the jail, to the chair, located in a room on the first floor in the north side of the building...".* [11] The above picture, with arrows, shows the northwest corner of the original jail house. To the left is the north side and it is likely Claude's execution took place in one of the rooms indicated by the arrows, and two months later, James Hughes' turn came to be executed. Though it is not possible to trace the actual rooms in which Claude was held or executed, still, it was within this building that a spectacular supernatural event in 1943 and the early part of 1944 took place to save two souls headed for not only mortal death, but very possibly eternal death.

Ceres Plantation, owned by U.G. Flowers, was the scene of the murder perpetrated by Claude Newman against Sid Cook. Sid Cook was born, raised and worked most of his life on Ceres Plantation, and it was also the home of Claude Newman for a couple of years after his grandmother, who raised Claude, married Cook. The marriage only lasted three years. On May 14, 2010, when Caritas Community members visited the locations connected to Claude Newman's life and death, while walking the grounds of Ceres Plantation, they approached an abandoned house. The only flowers seen in bloom, anywhere surrounding the house, was a wild rose bush. When they counted, they were amazed. Twelve red roses blooming: 12 Roses, 12 Stars. Our Lady often gives signs of confirmation of Her work for salvation of which this book is about. Our Lady didn't say without reason that **"…God wants to save you and sends you messages through men, nature, and so many things…"** (March 25, 1990) without actually doing so. More confirmation and another little interesting side note that the roses lead into: Claude's real mother's name was Floretta which means "little flower." St. Therese, also known as "the little flower," when a young girl, read of a condemned prisoner who was scheduled for execution, and who publicly denounced God. Therese was so distraught that this man would die and be condemned to hell, that she prayed and offered sacrifices everyday for his conversion. It appeared that all her prayers were in vain, when the day of his execution arrived and he mounted the steps to the hanging post. But, at the last moment, with the rope about his neck, he yelled for a priest, made his confession, and begged God's mercy on his soul. Therese was filled with joy. She became the spiritual mother of this prisoner, saving his soul from eternal death. It is an 'uncanny coincidence' that Claude Newman also received an extraordinary call that made him scream for a priest which resulted in him being saved miraculously by a mother.

When the Blessed Virgin Mary appeared to St. Catherine Laboure, July 18, 1830, amazingly, She was sitting down in a chair. That chair has been preserved all these years, and it is a moving experience for many of the visitors to Rue du Bac to see it, as it brings to life the apparitions in a very real sense. Shown here is the actual chair that is still present in the chapel. This picture was taken on May 15, 2010, by a Caritas community member who was sent to Rue du Bac for pictures and other research. It is located on the far right side of the Miraculous Medal Chapel only a few feet from where St. Catherine's miraculously perfectly preserved body can be seen. Even St. Catherine's 'blue' eyes slightly open can be seen. A Friend of Medjugorje spoke many times across France in the 1990s, and walked many times to this chapel for daily Mass and prayer with his wife. His devotion to the Miraculous Medal from these visits has always been strong.

This beautiful chapel, located at Rue du Bac in Paris, France, is where St. Catherine Laboure was given the grace to see the Virgin Mary in three separate apparitions. To the right of the main altar Our Lady appeared to St. Catherine while holding a globe that represented the world. A statue depicting Our Lady in this apparition is located in this spot, and just underneath is the incorrupt body of St. Catherine Laboure, the visionary of the Miraculous Medal. The chair Our Lady sat upon in the first apparition, pictured above, is located on the far right altar.

Pictured here is another famous chair, also connected to Our Lady, but it was a chair of death. This is the electric chair upon which convicted murderers, Claude Newman and James Hughes, ended their lives on earth.

From the Court Record of Claude Newman's Official Sentence:

"…It is thereupon considered by the Court and so ordered that for such his offense of Murder, the said defendant, Claude Newman, be taken to the County Jail of Warren County, Mississippi, and there safely kept in close confinement until the 14th day of May A.D. 1943, and that on said day and date and date to wit: the 14th day of May A.D. 1943, he, the said Claude Newman, the defendant herein, be taken by the proper authorities and in the Jail between legal hours, he, the defendant Claude Newman, then and there shall suffer death in the manner and form prescribed by law; that is to say, he, the said Claude Newman, shall suffer death in the County Jail of Warren County, Mississippi, on said date, within the hours aforesaid by the authorities and agencies authorized and created by law, causing to be administered and passed through the body of the person of the said Claude Newman, a current of electricity of sufficient intensity to cause his death, and the application and continuance of such current through the body of the person of him, the said Claude Newman, until he be dead; said electrocution to be carried out and performed as the law provides in such cases of Capital punishment." [12]

The original date assigned to Claude's execution was **May 14**, 1943. But his lawyer filed an appeal, and the case was heard again in October or November 1943. When the original verdict was affirmed, a new execution date was set for January 20, 1944.

By "holy coincidence," it was on **May 14**, 2010, when this picture was taken by a Caritas Community member who went to Vicksburg for documentation of Claude Newman's Story. We did not know, at the time, that May 14 held any significance. Confirmation of cooperation with Heaven. Our Lady said on July 24, 1989:

"…I need your cooperation…"

Original Miraculous Medal Back

Original Miraculous Medal Front

Vicksburg Evening Post: Friday, February 4, 1944

An article appeared in the *Vicksburg Evening Post* on February 4, 1944, describing Claude Newman's execution. The execution took place at 7:00 a.m. on February 4th, making it possible to include the story in the evening edition of the paper the same day. Within the article, there are details of Newman's life that coincide with Fr. O'Leary's story, including Newman's conversion to the Catholic faith while in jail and his comment that "he was ready to go" right before his execution in the electric chair.

Vicksburg Evening Post.

ASSOCIATED PRESS   VICKSBURG, MISSISSIPPI, FRIDAY, FEBRUARY 4, 1944   A. P.

CLAUDE NEWMAN EXECUTED TODAY

Pays with Life for Fatal Shooting of Sid Cook

Claude Newman, colored, aged 20 years, was electrocuted in the Warren county jail this morning at 7 o'clock. He died a few minutes after the current was applied. Newman walked from his cell, on the second floor of the jail, to the chair, located in a room on the first floor in the north side of the building, without assistance. He was preceded by Rev. Father O'Leary, of St. Mary's Catholic Church for colored.

Since being confined in the Warren jail, Newman had embraced the Catholic faith.

Newman's only comment prior to the execution was that he was ready to go.

Dr. A. J. Podesta, county physician, pronounced Newman dead, death being instantaneous.

His body was turned over to the People's Undertaking Company of Jackson.

Newman was executed for the fatal shooting of Sid Cook, colored, who resided on the U. G. Flowers place at Bovina. The shooting occurred the early part of 1943. He was arrested in Little Rock, Ark., and returned here for trial.

For his final meal last night, Newman ate a vegetable, beef dinner, and for dessert had coconut pie.

Newman was visited by relatives yesterday.

(Continued on Page Nine)

WASHINGTON, Feb. 4 — (A) Henry Cabot Lodge, Jr., resig today as senator from Massa setts in order to return to ac service as an army officer.

In a letter addressed to the state's presiding officer and by a clerk, the 41-year-old Lodge who holds a reserve commission a major, said he felt that in v of impending "large scale gr fighting" and his age, he c best serve his country as "a c bat soldier overseas."

Accordingly, he wrote: "I h by resign from the United St Senate."

Appointment of a successor in the hands of Republican ernor Leverett Saltonstall. Sai stall himself has been mention as a likely appointee to the

(Continued on Page Nine)

MUSTERING-OUT BILL IS SIGN

President Puts Final O On Pay Measure

WASHINGTON, Feb. 4— President Roosevelt signed t legislation providing musterin pay of $100 to $300 for mem of the armed services.

"At the same time, he called action on additional portions his program to "ease the pe of transition from military t vilian life."

Mr. Roosevelt mentioned s fically measures to let service continue their education, to vide social security credits for period of military service, en set up machinery for unem ment allowances.

The cemetery where Claude Newman was buried, known today as Beulah Cemetery and is located near Vicksburg, Mississippi. Fr. O'Leary relayed what happened to Claude's body after his execution on February 4, 1944:

"Just before Claude's death he asked me that I would be sure that he was given a decent and Christian burial. I took the body to church and buried him over the protest of many people. You see, many people in the south in those days had the idea if you died in an execution that you were absolutely condemned to hell. And they couldn't understand why his body was brought to a Catholic Church. We buried him with honor. We took the body to the cemetery. And as he requested, I ordered a stone to be made. It took about ten days to make the stone. And when it was made we went to the cemetery and could no longer find the grave. With bulldozers, the cemetery people had bulldozed the hill down behind Claude and had covered his grave under approximately 15 to 20 feet of earth. And so to this day we've never been able to find it. I guess maybe the Blessed Mother didn't want us to."[13]

Though his grave was never found, the overgrown cemetery surrounded by rolling hills, in a wooded area, covered with beautiful wild flowers is a fitting setting for Claude Newman's resting place. Had the Blessed Mother not intervened into Claude's life, he would have died a condemned, disgraced and forgotten soul and perhaps have remained that way for all eternity. Beulah Cemetery is a little piece of Heaven on earth, especially when one stands upon this ground, reflecting upon the mercy shown to Claude that saved his soul during the final months of his life.

CHAPTER SIX

What is in Control of Your Life?

Claude Newman's story is one which should motivate you to put Our Lady's November 27, 1989 Miraculous Medal Medjugorje message into action. Our Lady's words anew, about the Miraculous Medal, 'activates' what was asleep or lethargic in us. A desire is re-activated in this time to spread devotion to the Miraculous Medal, to encourage the carrying of it, and to pray for those who carry it to receive salvation, just as the murderer turned saint, Claude Newman did. And he passed salvation on to the reprobate who received salvation just before he was executed! And also, the other four men who took instruction and the women whom the nuns converted, giving instructions to at least one, Mildred James, who became Catholic just before her execution. We, too, are to pass on this grace of salvation. Is this November 27, 1989 commission of Our Lady to spread this devotion primary, even over the spreading of Her messages? No. Our Lady Herself said these messages contain...

January 25, 1987

"...a great plan for the salvation of mankind..."

Relaying to man these 'Words from Heaven' is the primary action of Heaven's plan both for our age and until the end of the world. But the Miraculous Medal is one of the spiritual tools, in harmony with Our Lady's messages, to be used to increase the number of conversions and miracles through this great plan for the salvation of the world!

In the writings of Maria Valtorta, the most known being The Poem of the Man-God as discussed in chapter two in which Our Lady said to Medjugorje visionary, Marija, **"One must read them,"** Valtorta relayed that Jesus said the time was coming when the great and final evangelization of the world would come. The evangelization would happen through new methods the world has never seen before. This was actually stated in her writing known as Notebooks, 1945–1950.

"He (Jesus) will raise up new evangelizers who will evangelize in His name. They will evangelize in a new way in keeping with the times, a new way which will not substantially change the eternal Gospel or the great Revelation, but will broaden, complete, and make them understandable and ac-

ceptable even to those who, on account of their atheism and their incredulity...cite the reason that 'they cannot believe (the truth)...to the new evangelizers. In reality, there already are, even if the world partly is unaware of them and partly attacks them. But they will be more and more numerous, and the world — after having overlooked or mocked or opposed them, when terror takes hold of the foolish who now deride the new evangelizers — will turn to them so that they will be strength, hope, and light in the darkness, horror, and tempest of ongoing persecution by the antichrists. For, if it is true that before the end of time more and more false prophets, servants of the anti-christ, will arise, it is equally true that Christ the Lord will set more and more of his servants against them, raising up new apostles in places where they are least expected."[14]

The new evangelizers will broaden, complete, and make the eternal Gospel "understandable and acceptable." Does Our Lady confirm in Her messages the above words of Maria Valtorta concerning the evangelists of today? Can we find in Her messages that She will call and raise up apostles who will bring new illumination to the eternal Gospel, just as Jesus did through His call to the apostles to do?

Our Lady said:

December 2, 2006

> **"... I call you to be my <u>apostles</u> of holiness so that, through you, the Good News may illuminate all those whom you will meet..."**

We live in an incredible moment in history. Need more evidence? Louis de Montfort was canonized a saint. This means what he said and witnessed with his life has credibility. St. Louis de Montfort said:

> *"...towards the end of the world...Almighty God and His holy Mother are to raise up saints who will surpass in holiness most other saints as much as the cedars of Lebanon tower above little shrubs.*

> *"These great souls filled with grace and zeal will be chosen to oppose the enemies of God who are raging on all sides. They will be exceptionally devoted to the Blessed Virgin. Illuminated by Her light, strengthened by Her spirit, supported by Her arms, sheltered under Her protection, they will fight with one hand and build with the other. With one hand they will give battle, overthrowing and*

*crushing heretics and their heresies, schismatics
and their schisms, idolaters and their idolatries,
sinners and their wickedness. With the other hand
they will build the temple of the true Solomon and
the mystical city of God, namely, the Blessed Virgin...*

*"They will be like thunderclouds flying through
the air at the slightest breath of the Holy Spirit.
Attached to nothing, surprised at nothing, they will
shower down the rain of God's word and of eternal life. They will thunder against sin; they will
storm against the world; they will strike down the
devil and his followers and for life and for death,
they will pierce through and through with the
two-edged sword of God's word all those against
whom they are sent by Almighty God.*

*"They will be true apostles of the latter times to
whom the Lord of Hosts will give eloquence and
strength to work wonders and carry off glorious
spoils from His enemies. They will sleep without
gold or silver and, more important still, without
concern in the midst of other priests, ecclesiastics
and clerics. Yet, they will have the silver wings of
the dove enabling them to go wherever the Holy
Spirit calls them, filled as they are, with the re-*

*solve to seek the glory of God and the salvation
of souls. Wherever they preach, they will leave .
behind them nothing but the gold of love, which is
the fulfillment of the whole law.*

*"They will have the two-edged sword of the Word
of God in their mouths and the bloodstained standard of the Cross on their shoulders. They will
carry the Crucifix in their right hand and the Rosary in their left, and the holy names of Jesus and
Mary on their heart.*

*"Mary scarcely appeared in the first coming of
Christ...But in the second coming of Jesus Christ,
Mary must be known and openly revealed by the
Holy Spirit so that Jesus may be known, loved and
served through Her."[15]*

There can be no doubt that Medjugorje is bringing forth this special time in the Church, and that it is
through Our Lady's messages that She will raise up the
saints and apostles. The mission of Caritas of Birmingham has taken this to heart. Through various innovative
ways of evangelization, we've presented Our Lady's
messages to modern man, placing them as a 'template'
over many different things, technologies, economics,
subject matters, worldviews, etc., to bring Our Lady's

slant to that area of culture in order to use it as a hook to catch more fish for conversion, just as Jesus once told His twelve apostles to become fishers of men. Her messages give modern man the correct Biblical worldview over everything. Modern man cannot relate to ancient writings of the sacred text found in Scripture, as today's man discounts their words as antiquated. Our Lady comes veiled, clothed, only Her face and hands showing, anciently dressed according to modern man's standards, but with words that bridge the divide. Visionary Marija has said Our Lady's messages are for today's man to help him understand the Bible.

We, at Caritas, have often used crisis or things 'seemingly' totally unrelated to Our Lady's messages, to introduce many souls to Our Lady. These things have included every kind of subject on the earth. Divorce, finance, sickness, material possessions and their loss, laws, destroyed families, hurricanes and disasters, the environment, new technologies, the government and on and on. Caritas has experienced beautiful and abundant fruit by taking all 'these things' that satan is often directly or indirectly involved with and, through Our Lady's messages, finding a solution. By putting the messages as a template over the crisis, topic, etc., to discern the spiritual decision or directive that should be walked, it purifies man's heart in the use of 'these things' and the events that led to a negative consequence. And so the thing or crisis that was used by satan to hurt someone's spiritual life becomes sanctified and instead cures one's spiritual life, leading to conversion and salvation for the soul. Our Lady says:

February 25, 1990

> "...do not allow satan to come into your life through those 'things' that hurt both you and your spiritual life..."

We are to change things that hurt our lives to things that help towards eternal gain.

January 25, 2009

> "...for all worldly things to be a help for you to draw you closer to God the Creator..."

Our Lady said:

July 25, 1988

> "...Everything you do and everything you possess give over to God so that He can take control in your life as King of all that you possess..."

Things of the earth were made by the Creator. Do you use them in helping yourself and others gain eternal salvation? Or are these things used by satan to hurt your spiritual life and lead you towards eternal damnation?

With Our Lady's words of November 27, 1989, and Her overall messages for the world's salvation, comes an incredible thing you can do, along with living Her basic messages of prayer, peace, fasting, and penance. It is Our Lady who has pointed very clearly to one of those major things of which She said satan makes use of so he can:

"...come into your life through those things that hurt both you and your spiritual life..." February 25, 1990

Money!

CHAPTER SEVEN

Who would God say your god is?

Incredibly, Our Lady reveals Her spiritual and physical strategy, that one can do to defeat satan in the world by defeating satan in the heart of man, in a message She gave on August 5, 1986:

"Read each Thursday the Gospel of Matthew, where it is said: 'No one can serve two masters... You cannot serve God and money.'"

By this message, Our Lady wants to erase the heart, to clean it and give it a new way in all that has afflicted it. Our Lady said:

February 2, 2008

"...I am with you. As a mother, I am gathering you, because I desire to erase from your hearts what I see now. Accept the love of my Son and erase fear, pain, suffering and disappointment from your heart..."

We can find in the family today, fear, pain, suffering and disappointment. There are millions of wounded hearts within the structure of the family today. What is the primary cause of divorce today? It is commonly known among those who are involved in marriage counseling, and it is our experience as well, that the number one reason for divorce is finances. Yes, money. The reason is not solely related to the lack of money or not having enough money, because just as many people divorce who have money. 'It' is the desire for money and the 'things' money buys. Money is definitely the number one reason for the destruction of the family. Medjugorje visionary Ivan said:

> *"Look at the responsibility of parents. Often they are so interested in material things, peer pressure among friends, or personal gratification in each other to the exclusion of children both born and unborn...Often there is little or no love between a husband and a wife. Often there is little respect. When that happens, the spirit of the children is sickened. Then satan has immense power in the family. Where there is great love of luxury, or ease, or prestige, or professional accomplishment, satan has much power."[16]*

Our Lady said on June 25, 1989:

"Pray because you are in great temptation and danger because the world and material goods lead you into slavery. satan* is active in this plan. I want to help each of you in prayer. I am interceding to my Son for you."

Our Lady said:

November 2, 2009

"...I ask of you to sincerely look into your hearts and to see how much you love Him (God the Father)**. Is He the last to be loved? Surrounded by material goods, how many times have you betrayed, denied and forgotten Him? My children, do not deceive yourselves with worldly goods... Thank you."**

---

* satan does not deserve respect or honor when references are made to him. Most of you have probably noticed for years we have not capitalized his name because we refuse to give him this honor or recognition. Why should the application of grammar rules apply to him who has an insatiable desire to be exalted, even above God? We refrain in our references and writings from giving him the same stature afforded even a dog's name, which would be capitalized. We are not radical in that we don't tell others they must do the same. It's up to each individual to decide for themselves. For the harm he has done to man, whom he despises, we will not grant him that which is even reserved for a dog.

Our Lady said on March 25, 1996:

> **"Dear children! I invite you to decide again to love God above all else. In this time, when due to the spirit of consumerism, one forgets what it means to love and to cherish true values, I invite you again, little children, to put God in the first place in your life. Do not let satan attract you through material things but, little children, decide for God who is freedom and love. Choose life and not death of the soul..."**

Interestingly enough, statistics are showing that because of the hard economic times, divorces, while still cancerously high, are taking place less today because couples can't afford to get divorced. Aaron Dishon, a certified family law specialist in Irvine, California said:

> *"A divorce could cost anywhere from the low-end of $50,000 to a high-end of $200,000 or more. These days, many people can't even afford to even maintain one home, let alone two homes with two mortgages or rents, utilities and all the other costs of maintaining a household. Some couples are so hard-hit by financial problems that they divorce, but stay in the same house and many others are trying harder to stay together."*[17]

Bonnie Booder, divorce attorney in Phoenix, Arizona, stated:

> *"One out of every two clients is seeking consultations because they can't afford to get divorced. They want to know what other options they might have. I tell them about the process, about the cost, and what a reasonable outcome might be. And once they hear the cost, and especially how you have to duplicate two households on the same money that currently funds one household, they try to think about some other options."* [18]

Research has shown that with couples who were experiencing difficult marriages but who decide to stick it out, after five years of staying together the majority of the couples experience renewed love, happiness and contentment in their marriage again.[19] So, it would seem, that one of the 'fruits' of the economic downturn is that more families are staying intact and are 'working harder' to find ways to stay together. God's corrective measures are at play in this. In order to keep their marriages together, many couples are seeking advice in how to handle their finances because this is where so much of their conflict arises, through the mismanagement and/or inordinate want of money.

Virtually everything in life involves and connects to
money: luxuries, ease, prestige, professional accomplish-
ments, etc. You may have an inordinate desire such as
buying a car you can't afford, gluttony, being miserly
and hoarding what you have, etc. But, at the root of all
of these things, is the desire, the **love** for money. 1 Timothy 6:10 states:

"For the love of money is the root of all evils."

Claude Newman, through his want and 'love' for money,
killed a man.

Therefore, this does not mean money itself is evil. It
means the root of the tree of evil always involves the
'love' of money. Evil is driven by the love of money.
Money is exchanged for 'things.' So in reality, the lust
for things is rooted to money that buys it. But again, it
is not to money itself, but to the desire for money. Money can also be the root to grow a tree that good fruit
blooms from. It is why Our Lady said:

January 25, 2009

**"...for all worldly things to be a help for you to
draw you closer to God the Creator..."**

Since Scripture states that 'love' of money is the root
of all evils, and we, today, are living in an evil age, it

behooves us to look more closely at the system of exchange in our world today, exchange being the purpose for which money exists. We exchange money to receive goods and services. God, as the Creator, created gold and silver, which historically have always been used primarily for the purpose of exchange to receive 'things', or rather goods or services. This exchange cannot be without God's design, as the all-knowing God would certainly know what everything would be used for which He created it. This, therefore, brings us to three important revelations in regards to Our Lady's apparitions, and as always with Our Lady, there is 'three'.   Pray, Pray, Pray.

But what does all this have to do with spreading the Miraculous Medal and Our Lady's message? Still more must be explained first.

CHAPTER EIGHT

One Master
6/24   6:24   6/24

Our Lady wanted Her anniversary apparition to be celebrated on June 25 every year, yet it was not Her first apparition. Our Lady first appeared the day before June 25. Many are aware of Our Lady's symbolic gesture of the first apparition being on the feast day of St. John the Baptist, the Proclaimer of the Messiah. It is clear Our Lady is coming back to the world, 2000 years later, for the purpose to reintroduce the world to Her Son. The intent of that first apparition is clear for the believer and, again, many are aware of this. As already written, Our Lady is with us for the purpose to **erase** that which blocks us from Her Son.

February 2, 2008

> **"...I am with you...to <u>erase</u> from your hearts what I see now. Accept the love of my Son and <u>erase</u> fear, pain, suffering and disappointment from your heart..."**

Erase what? Erase also the source of what most often causes fear, pain, suffering and disappointment.

Our Lady said on August 5, 1986:

> **"Read each Thursday the Gospel of Matthew, where it is said: 'No one can serve two masters... You cannot serve God and money.'"**

When She spoke these words, She revealed a primary strategy of where Her attack could make the most radical change in the world. We are beginning to 'see' this significance, as we begin to understand more deeply the reason for Our Lady's coming.

With the event of Our Lady's apparitions in Medjugorje, as the years pass by and events unfold, we begin to understand the prophetic nature of Our Lady's words and actions, of which, without the passage of time, we could not have known otherwise. For instance, the above August 5, 1986 message is given on Our Lady's birthday, August 5.* We know Our Lady has been given

---

* On August 5, 1984, Our Lady Queen of Peace of Medjugorje revealed to the visionaries and to the village of Medjugorje that August 5 was Her real birthday. The Church recognizes and celebrates Our Lady's birthday on September 8. We are in no way usurping the Church's September 8 celebration. We believe when Heaven ordains it, the Church will recognize August 5 as Our Lady's real birthday. Until then, we believe Our Lady is deserving of two birthday celebrations.. For more information about August 5 being Our Lady's birthday, order the booklet *"August 5th, What are You Doing for Her Birthday?"* on medjugorje.com or by calling Caritas of Birmingham, 205-672-2000, ext. 315 24 hrs.

gifts, graces She has asked for on our behalf to help us. The message of the Gospel of Matthew, "God and money," is a primary strategy of attack against the woes of the world. The fact Our Lady gives this on Her birthday prophetically tells us, as time passes, how important the Universal Church will hold August 5 in comparison to Christmas. Only when the Holy Spirit is ready to give insights about certain revelations* at the proper time, will we see what was there in front of us all along. Therefore, **6/24** or June 24, the date of Our Lady's first apparition in Medjugorje is a revelation over and beyond John the Baptist's feast day. There is also another purpose to this date, a major revelation concerning Her apparitions, to help us recognize part of Her strategy to 'erase' from our hearts that which is the root of many of our sins and consequential problems we have inherited.

One plan of Our Lady to turn hearts away from an inordinate love of money and towards Jesus as Our Lord, was to have the parish 'gather', **"...I gather you..."** April 25, 1988, to read every week the particular Scripture verse concerning serving God or money.

---

* For the theologically inclined, the author understands all public revelation ceased with the death of the last apostle. Our Lady's messages of Medjugorje are private revelation. The mentioning of revelation is not in the context of public revelation, but rather insights that are revealed through the private revelations of Our Lady's plans and messages of Medjugorje, all of which help us have greater insight into public revelation.

As already stated, the first reason for the break up of the family is the seeking after and the inordinate desire for money and what it buys. A family is a small civilization. Break down that sacred institution, through the inordinate desire for things and the love of money, and you will, as visionary Ivan warns, plague the family with innumerable problems because that is the root of the problem. By Our Lady leading the parish to pray every Thursday, the Scripture from Matthew speaks very strongly that She wants to attack the root of the world's problems. Yes, it is sin, of course, but She shows us, through reading this Scripture, what She wants to erase in our hearts. Our Lady said:

March 18, 1985

> **"...Right now <u>many</u> are <u>greatly</u> seeking money, not only in the parish, but in the whole world..."**

Our Lady is clearly showing the world that the first root to its sin is materialism in which, as She said, we forget what is most important. As you already read, Our Lady said on March 25, 1996:

> **"...due to the spirit of consumerism, one forgets what it means to love and to cherish true values..."**

USA Today, in an April 2010 issue, printed the results of a study showing women who wait to become mothers until they are into their thirties or later, will make more money, as they can return to the job market after the baby is born, having already established their careers. Women who have children at a younger age put themselves under the "motherhood penalty," as they do not develop job skills, complete their education, and/or lack the experience of women who put their careers first. The report conveys that the wise mother 'waits' and makes it, while the other is foolish because she'll have less money and be poor — hence, the "motherhood penalty."[20] What does Our Lady think about this? You already know the answer, for Our Lady said 'many' are 'greatly' seeking money throughout the whole world, forgetting **"...what it means to love and to cherish true values..."**

So can we now understand Our Lady's reason for very directly and very pointedly wanting this Scripture **'read by everyone' in the whole parish every Thursday?** Because serving money, the love thereof, is the primary root of evil. Isn't this why She came June 24, 1981? To erase from our hearts what cannot coexist with Jesus because you can serve but only one master: God or money? Didn't Our Lady warn the parish and the whole world?

March 18, 1985

"...Right now many are greatly seeking money, not only in the parish, but in the whole world..."

Because we believed Her words, we, at Caritas, have read for years this Scripture verse on our grounds every Thursday. This led to a grace that gave birth to Caritas beginning a weekly radio show entitled *Mejanomics** based on those principles Our Lady is teaching. We chose to broadcast every Thursday, and to begin the program with reading the Bible passage, *"You cannot serve two masters...,"* simply by obedience to the message, because Our Lady said this passage is to be read every Thursday. Starting *Mejanomics* was a bold decision because we are very aware of an element of resistance from narrow minded mentalities of some in the Medjugorje movement who reject that Our Lady would involve Herself in the money matters of the world. A Medjugorje radio program about your financial problems, future security, your protection in the present economic system, etc., called *Mejanomics* is our response to Our Lady's request to read this Scripture of Matthew.

---

* See Glossary for further explanation.

We have no problem bringing this to fruition, but we know there are those who do not grasp the significance of Our Lady's messages in regard to this, and that they would revert to slandering us, as has often happened when we implement Our Lady's messages. However, we do not care what some who work in the Medjugorje movement may think, because from Our Lady's own lips the world has fallen into slavery through the present economic order, or better said, 'disorder,' and so this path was easily discernible.

We have discovered repeatedly that where we implement boldly Our Lady's message, She will reveal things about them, heretofore unknown to us or the Medjugorje movement. We were very surprised as this is exactly what happened after broadcasting *Mejanomics* for several months and reading the Scripture passage every Thursday. An unknown secret was revealed that had been before our very eyes for almost three decades but enlightenment was only given when we became more serious in promoting this message ourselves. It was a revelation that came to light only after we, at Caritas, stepped forward to broadcast this Scripture passage to the whole world to encourage its reading and application into life, as the Caritas Community was doing for years. Our Lady made known to us that

Her first apparition of June 24 **(6/24)**, was connected
to the Bible passage, particularly the verse concerning
serving two masters, in Matthew. Our Lady said:

March 1, 1984

> **"Each Thursday, read again the passage of Mat-
> thew 6:24–34, before the Most Blessed Sacra-
> ment, or if it is not possible to come to church, do
> it with your family."**

What? Did you catch that? Matthew 6:24! Incredibly, it is the match for the first apparition of 6/24.
Though we had read this Scripture of Matthew hundreds of times on Thursdays, the chapter and verse **6:24**
remained hidden until we took our years of Thursday
readings and made a decision to introduce new people
to this request of Our Lady and reintroduce it to those
who no longer did this throughout the world through
Mejanomics. It is an incredible revelation. The importance of **6:24** is such that Our Lady wanted it to be read
weekly. The importance of **6:24** is such that it is to be
read in front of the Blessed Sacrament! The importance
of **6:24** is such that if you cannot read it in front of the
Blessed Sacrament, Our Lady says you are to read it in
your family every Thursday! Matthew **6:24**–34! Our
Lady came to the earth on June 24 or 6/24, with the in-

tention to erase the errors of our hearts that fruit into
fear, pain, suffering, and disappointment. For this Scripture passage to be Matthew 6:24, and that it is a primary
request of Our Lady that we read it each week, cannot
be a simple coincidence with it connecting to the date
of Her first apparition, using the same numerical digits.
Rather, She gave it with the intention for this connection to become a special focus and for us to recognize its
significance and the **greatness** of the Scripture's message
of Matthew 6:24–34. It was Our Lady who pinpointed
directly the 6:24 verse with particular emphasis.

August 5, 1986

> **"Read each Thursday the Gospel of Matthew,
> where it is said: 'No one can serve two masters…
> You cannot serve God and money.'"**

Can one think the date Our Lady came to the world
on 6/24, and Matthew 6:24 happened without it being
ordained — Our Lady, being all wisdom, God being all
knowing? Would one think Our Lady and God had
a conversation, *"Hey, what do you know! My first apparition date was 6/24 and what I asked to be read every
Thursday, Matthew 6:24 is the same. How about that for
a coincidence; what a strange coincidence."* On a human
level, man often makes 15 out of 1. But when it is to the

'greatness' of the message, the living of the profoundness of the message, man wants to confine Our Lady's
works and actions only to 1 out of 1. Minimizing the
apparitions and Our Lady's messages, man's puny mind
cannot fathom God's simplicity, making 'many' out of
one, but when it comes to himself, has no trouble in
very complex ways, making 'many' out of one. This 6:24
verse of serving two masters was something Our Lady
asked to be read every Thursday, but the connection She
revealed between the date of Her first apparition and
this chapter and verse from Matthew remained hidden
for 29* years of apparitions. It was not revealed until
Her messages were implemented to do this on a worldwide scale, through the *Mejanomics* Radio program.
What was in front of us the whole time was suddenly
seen, simply by doing and living what She asked us to
do and live. This should be the impetus to seek first the
Kingdom of God to see what still lies hidden that God
wants to reveal to us through Our Lady's messages.
Our Lady's first apparition 6/24; Matthew 6:24. But it
was written that Our Lady works in three's. Is there another 6/24 revelation? Our Lady said:

---

* As of June 2010. This book being written March–May 2010.

May 2, 2009

**"...You are permitting sin to overcome you more
and more. You are permitting it to master you
and to take away your power of discernment..."**

One can discern that the present economic order is
based on a lie. An economy based on debt, where people borrow to have immediate gratification in reality is a
system where people sell themselves into slavery. Norm
Franz said:

> *"Gold is the money of kings;*
> *Silver is the money of gentlemen;*
> *Barter is the money of peasants;*
> *But debt is the money of slaves."[21]*

It is absolutely ludicrous and an incredible lie that our
individual viability and security, as well as the world's
economy, can be based on debt. It is insane to think, as
promoted, that for the economy to recover, banks must
start lending and people must start borrowing! Debt is
contrary to Biblical principles and the world has taken a
wayward direction in the way it operates today. Therefore, it is God who will bring us to a new understanding,
spearheaded by Our Lady. It is Her messages which will
navigate us back to the right path, but are you open to
this? Can you see this?

If you **pray**, if you foster **peace**, if you **fast**, if you do **penance**, your eyes will open and what you could not see you will see. The economic order, as we have known it, is on the brink of destruction. **It will not be saved from this destruction.** Because 'many' of the world, including many in the Church, do not pray, do not have peace, do not fast, and do not do penance, they believe our economic system will recover. It will not, and God out of mercy is letting it bounce up and down to give the elect the grace for what Our Lady said on September 25, 2008, to:

"...make good use of this time..."

We are being granted a period of grace to prepare the heart and soul, first, spiritually to grow in holiness and, second, **physically to grow in security**, a new security through a new special way, a new way of living life which God desires for us. Physical security? Many see God's only interest for us is spiritual. Not true! God wants the good and well-being of His children. A people are not so much protected by their armaments, as they are by their way of life. When the way of life goes wayward from God's Commandments, people lose not only their spiritual well-being, but their physical well-being as well. So while many cling to the hope the economic system will fully recover, the moral condition

of the world is the stone wall which will prevent its recovery.

It is necessary to explain further why 'only a few'
believe the economic system is 'not' going to get better
and why 'many' believe one, two, ten years from now,
the economic system will recover. The camp who grows
in the living of the four basic messages Our Lady gave
in the beginning of Her apparitions, **prayer, peace, fasting, and penance** can see that Our Lady is coming to
the world to change it. *For Our Lady to change a world
gone radically against God's ways can only mean that the
world must radically change to go back to God's ways.
Let it be understood: life as we know it, the economic
order as we know it, is going to go through a radical
transformation away from the way of life as we know it.*
Those who see the economic order recovering cannot
see what is clearly in front of them. They are as those
who believe they see, yet are blind. In these 29 years of
daily apparitions, Our Lady has denounced consumerism, materialism, things hurtful to the spiritual life, excessive pleasures, vanity, frivolity, and on and on. These
things will not coexist with Her 'wants'. What are Her
wants? They are God's wants! What does God want?
Our Lady tells us what God's desire is.

June 25, 2007

"...God desires to convert the entire world and to call it to salvation..."

CHAPTER NINE

It's Localization, Not Globalization!

The economic system of usury (usury is explained fully in a later chapter) and the debtors' participation in usury has matured in fullness. Man is soiled with discontentment, desires, and greed. This corrupt system, infecting the whole world, will not and cannot coexist equally with Our Lady's presence upon the earth. One, and only one, will triumph. Who will you bet your money on? Those who love money will bet theirs on the present economic order. Those few who understand money in the Biblical sense will bet theirs against the present economic disorder and for what Our Lady is revealing about a new way of life that is coming.

The system of globalization and the economic order will be the tool the anti-christ will make use of, as the book of Revelation foretells. Darkness drives this system toward the goal of being interconnected, for the sake of unifying a system that can be centrally controlled. Globalization is not of God. Localization is of God. The small village, small community is where people can know each other, care for each other. With globalization, you become faceless. The mega parishes, the mega churches today, both Catholic and Protestant, are not community. They cannot be real communities by fact of the sheer numbers involved. It is why Jesus built His Church on His twelve apostles, His disciples, along with some Holy women, probably numbering no more than a hundred people who were intimately involved together. All militaries of the world know their platoons cannot number much more than one hundred men. After that, cohesiveness breaks down and disorder rises. Community wanes in large numbers as people begin to form cliques. It is why globalization will lead to disaster and localization will lead to a way of life.

Medjugorje consists of five small separate hamlets. The hamlet of Medjugorje is where the church is located. Bijakovici is at the foot of Apparition Mountain. Miletina is at the foot of Cross Mountain, and the remaining two are Vionica and Surmanci. The book, The Tipping Point, relays the magic number where community and unity is lost is 150 people. Having learned this truth, the religious community the Hutterites, once they reach the point of having 150 members in one community, will have some members break off to form a neighboring community.[22] They have survived and thrived through this insight that should teach us something. Has Our Lady come to prophetically tell us what the future looks like?

In Medjugorje, in the beginning days, many saw a strange occurrence on Cross Mountain. Some even saw it from afar. One of those who witnessed it was the visionary Marija's brother, Andrija. He said that he and others saw the whole of the sky over Cross Mountain, covered in what looked like a white veil, except one could see through it. Through the veil, they could see a small church with four or five houses around it. The four or five houses were surrounded with green fields. Then there was another church with four or five houses around it, surrounded by green fields. And then another and another repeat of the scene. When Andrija was asked how many, he said hundreds of churches were surrounded the same way. How long did the vision last? Fifteen minutes. Did they just stay in the sky? No, the little village churches were descending to the earth (on Cross Mountain) very slowly. Through the years, Andrija was asked about this several times, and what he thought it meant. He would say, *"It meant what I saw."*[23]

What did Marija's brother see? How should we understand it? The Community of Caritas is a prophetic community, a "prototype" of what the future will look like. How can that be said? The following is taken from the book <u>Words From Heaven</u>®.

December 13, 1988

> *When Our Lady appeared, She conveyed to Marija Her desire to start a community at the site. Marija turned to the host in whose house she was living and said to him immediately after the apparition,*
>
> *"Our Lady wants to start a community here."*
>
> *The husband and wife were deeply struck by these words.*

The resulting Community of Caritas continues to evolve in present time to show and point the way for future time. Our Lady, through Marija's apparitions, has continually formed and shaped Her community with Her words and actions, especially in Her apparitions when Marija stays with the community in Alabama.

What Andrija, Marija's brother saw was small villages in numbers where people could be community. The plans of darkness are the opposite. For instance, you have probably heard of Sustainable Development. Part of the plan of Sustainable Development and Smart Growth; is to force people off their property and into 'infill zones' of tightly packed, populated areas.[24]

These infill zones are to hold the greatest concentration of people as possible to get them off the land, in order to supposedly protect the religion of ecology, while the real truth of darkness is to control people and their beliefs. Why? Beliefs are as dangerous as ideas, particularly Christian principled ideas when they lead man towards his quest of God, freedom, and liberty. They are dangerous to those who seek control of the masses. Stalin said:

> *"Ideas are far more powerful than guns. We don't allow our enemies to have guns, why should we allow them to have ideas?"*[25]

Therefore, the move to force people into 'infill zones' is a main thrust of Sustainable Development and carefully implemented plans are in place throughout our country and the world to achieve this.* It is a main element of United Nation's Agenda 21, a plan for globalization resulting from the dark motives in the heart of man. It contrasts with localization which gives man autonomy, and thereby freedom to self-govern his affairs, representative of the Light of Liberty and Goodness of God. What has all this got to do with what is being written in regards to use of money? To broaden your understanding of the principles of light, principles which teach a measured life, bringing freedom. The principles of darkness teach principles of an unmeasured life, bringing slavery.

Byzantine's economy lasted 800 years.[27] Why was that? Because Byzantine's economy was backed by gold. It could not expand beyond the amount of gold they held. The eight hundred years of stability was an incredible feat, bound by the limitation set by the amount of precious metals they held. As long as they backed their economy with the exact 'measure' they had in gold, the system was stable. This system puts a limitation on the economy of how much it can expand,

---

* "Sustainable Development and Smart Growth root back to United Nations' Agenda 21 documents that reveal a grand plan to remove not only individual rights to own private property, but entails controlling virtually every aspect of individuals lives and major population control, birth control, abortion, movement of population, etc." [26]

yet gives a stable economy because the gold or what the gold backs has real worth.

Silver, throughout history, has also been used as the exchange for goods and services. These two precious metals, gold and silver, did not come to be used for monetary exchange through man one day deciding, *"Well, we've got quartz, copper, gold, diamonds, silver, etc. Let's just pick one!"* Gold and silver came to be naturally used by man for this purpose of exchange because the Creator created these elements to have this major purpose, among their other uses. Through human reason, man saw their rarity and their remarkable traits, but it was God who made them rare and gave them the traits which navigated man to discover their ordained use.

Within the natural law of creation, things work on their own toward the natural result of their use. When we try to go against natural law, we will always end up in disaster and a crash. This is why Our Lady has many messages about God the Creator and going out into nature. In nature, we will observe God, His natural ways, His laws, and we will conform to them. And with good will, following the 'measured' limit programmed in nature, we, thereby, will be stable. Throughout history, gold and silver have been the backing behind paper currency, and when not, the currency failed. This is the case today in our economy. To always be breaking the boundaries of the fixed measurements gold and silver provided, going beyond the amount in reserve to back up the currency, means certain destruction. Nature has within itself a built in self-correction to return the world and man back to the boundaries God programmed into creation. This correction is why it is said that nature itself defends God when man lives without the measurements of limitation found throughout creation.

If this is hard for you to grasp, here is a more simple way to put it. If man cuts trees faster than they can grow, the natural penalty is that wood becomes more expensive as it depletes. Measured cutting of trees at the replacement growth rate, ensures a steady price and stable supply; that is, a measured use of what God supplied, according to the principles of measurement the Creator programmed into creation. God is an abundant God when we live a measured way of life. God's creation will turn on us when we turn to unmeasured living, or against the natural law. This applies to everything in life, in every form. Darkness, therefore, is always saying if it feels good, do it; if you want it, take it; if you have a desire, fulfill it. A 'non'-measured life, without limitations, will always lead to a very restricted measured life with choking limitations. We are inheriting in the world today the fruits of unmeasured living, in our lives, institutions, governments, politics, economies and relationships, inheriting all the problems of culture all across the world. And all are rooted to Matthew 6:24, where the love for money is the root of this evil in which true values have been lost and are no longer recognized.

Man's insatiable appetite for living beyond the measured Christian principles of what God has programmed for him, is why the want of money has developed to the point of enslaving and bringing down the whole world's culture.

CHAPTER TEN

The Bet is On

So how are we supposed to live in a culture driving the car we are in that is about to crash? The crash being the total collapse of the present economic order? Simply get out of the car when it slows down around a curve. You may get scratched and bruised up, but you are going to get killed if you are still in the car when it crashes. That means, get out by living measured. Have no debt, down size if necessary to get out of debt. He who lives by paying up front for what he acquires is within the measure of what God provides for him. Whereas, the man who borrows to get what he wants, going into debt, is living beyond the measure of what God has provided for him. Which one do you want to be, the one who lives beyond the prescribed measurement, staying in the crashing car, or the one who begins living by the prescribed measurement, who jumps out of the car? By jumping out, you'll get hurt a little. You will have to do a lot of things you might not want to do. But by changing what you seek and instead seeking first the measured living found in Matthew's 6:24–34, seeking first the way of the Kingdom of God, your needs will be met. Our Lady prophetically, through Scripture, tells you what will happen.

> *Even though most all have read and heard the following before, do not skim or skip through these Scriptures. Rather, enter into it and penetrate its message for you and the whole world.*

Matthew 6:24–34

"No one can serve two masters. He will either hate one and love the other, or be devoted to one and despise the other. You cannot serve God and mammon. Therefore, I tell you, do not worry about your life, what you will eat or drink, or about your body, what you will wear. Is not life more than food and the body more than clothing? Look at the birds in the sky; they do not sow or reap, they gather nothing into barns, yet your Heavenly Father feeds them. Are not you more important than they? Can any of you by worrying add a single moment to your life-span? Why are you anxious about clothes? Learn from the way the wild flowers grow. They do not work or spin. But I tell you that not even Solomon in all his splendor was clothed like one of them. If God so clothes the grass of

the field, which grows today and is thrown into the oven tomorrow, will He not much more provide for you, O you of little faith? So do not worry and say, 'What are we to eat?' or 'What are we to drink?' or 'What are we to wear?' All these things the pagans seek. Your Heavenly Father '<u>knows</u>' that you need them all. '<u>But</u>' seek '<u>first</u>' the kingdom of God and His righteousness, and <u>all these things will be given you besides</u>. Do not worry about tomorrow; tomorrow will take care of itself. Sufficient for a day is its own evil."

So, by not seeking what the culture seeks, but rather seeking first the Kingdom of God, <u>all</u> these things will be given to you besides! God is not telling us to live on the streets, nor does He want us to. Medjugorje visionary, Ivanka, said Our Lady told her that God Himself wills the discomfort of none of His children.[28] He is telling us, "If you become mine, with your whole heart and soul, I will provide for you." When you focus on seeking first the kingdom and incorporating righteousness in your life, you will experience the fruit of God giving you all these things besides. It's God's will to provide for you! All you have to do is seek God and ride in the car He is driving to arrive at a safe place — His car, His means of a way of life and His method of exchange.

Is this writing saying, *"If I have little money, God will still provide me land and a house? With little money?"* Yes, that is what is being said if these are your needs. But you cannot sit around making foolish decisions and wait for it to fall out of the sky. Jesus said, **"Look at the birds in the sky; they do not sow or reap, they gather nothing into barns, yet your Heavenly Father feeds them."** But understand this: those birds have to get out of their nests early and work to go find the worm God provides for them. Starting at daybreak, they have to labor to find the sticks and straw God provides to build a nest. They have to be tireless in the activity of gathering food for their little ones in their nests. Observe what God provides, but be mindful of what is required to acquire what God provides. The following, a poem from the Great Depression era, speaks of this truth, just as Jesus telling His parables to teach a lesson, did the same.

The Rooster and the Hen

Said the little Red Rooster, "Believe me, things are tough.
Seems the worms are getting scarcer and I cannot find enough.
What's become of all those fat ones? It's a mystery to me.
There were thousands through that rainy spell,
But now where can they be?"

But the old black hen who heard him didn't grumble or complain.
She had lived through lots of dry spells,
She had lived through floods of rain.
She picked a new and undug spot. The ground was hard and firm.
"I must go to the worms," she said. "The worms won't come to me."

The rooster vainly spent his day through habit by the ways,
Where fat, round worms had passed in squads back in the rainy days.
When nightfall found him supper-less, he growled in accents rough.
"I'm hungry as a fowl can be, conditions sure are tough."

But the old black hen hopped to her perch
And dropped her eyes to sleep.
And murmured in a drowsy tone, "Young man hear this and weep.
I'm full of worms and happy for I've eaten like a pig.
The worms were there as always, but boy I had to dig."

All you have to do is seek the Kingdom of God and then all will be given to you. When you apply the Christian principles into your life, the Christian principles of living in moderation, and apply Our Lady's messages, God will guide you, as a Provider, meeting and exceeding your needs.

Remember, your inordinate wants make you poor. Also, an entitlement mentality will lead to poverty. Many think they are poor. **One is only poor when one lacks what is necessary to live**. Many who believe they are poor are really enslaved by the culture of debt. You can break these shackles as the following testimony shows. We, at Caritas, have received many testimonies through the years by guiding people through Our Lady's messages. God has blessed with land, homes, and security those who had very little money, yet through their working hard and with faith in walking the way of God, He provides. Sacrifices are required in seeking the Kingdom. These sacrifices are bumps and scratches that come from jumping out of the system, 'the car' which is going to crash, in which most everyone else is following by riding along. The following testimony sent to Caritas shows what God can do for those who choose a harder way, but a better and more secure way, resulting in God providing:

Dear Caritas,   *February, 2010*

My husband and I were married in 1979, we were young and in love, our parents did not encourage us to get married. Neither one of us had a college education nor a really good job. We felt a need to get married; we had a full Mass and dedicated our marriage to Our Lady, 90 percent of the people in attendance at our wedding were not Catholic, they did not understand what was taking place. One and a half years later we were living in a very small apartment with our first child. Life was full of struggles.

Five years after we were married, we inherited $10,000. This seemed like a lot of money. We wanted to be sure to spend it wisely, so we prayed to make the right choice. My husband decided we needed to purchase property to make a start; we wanted to build a house. He asked me to put an ad in the paper. The ad stated…"Family has $4000. Would like to purchase property for house or mobile home." We prayed and we received phone call after phone call from people who wanted us to use the $4000 as a down payment. We *had decided that if we were going to be able to move onto the property, we would only be able to spend $4000 on the property. I really did not think we would be able to find anything for this amount of money. Then one day, a lady called and told me that she had an acre and a half. It had city water and electricity, and get this, she only wanted $3000. I could not believe what I was hearing. The property was beautiful. We were able to purchase the property, and put in all the utilities, septic tank, culvert, etc. We then searched for a mobile home. We put another ad in the paper and waited. "Family would like to purchase mobile home." We looked at many mobile homes, most were falling apart. We were about to give up and we had one last call. The lady wanted $1000 more than we had. The mobile home was an old, well built mobile home. She happened to be a co-worker of my mother-in-law. She allowed us to pay it out over a year. We lived for over 12 years in the mobile home. It was more like camping to some people. Our little mobile home was heated with wood heat. We had no* *air-conditioning. I had to hang up all of our clothes to dry as we had no clothes dryer and a dishwasher was beyond me. Many people thought we were crazy. I heard many times, "I just would not live like that." We raised our two boys in this little mobile home. The roar of crickets and frogs at night always sound like home. We thanked God for our home and our property. We felt it was Heaven sent and blessed.*

Life was full of all sorts of struggles, struggles many families did not experience. We were blessed again and inherited more money. This time we wanted to build a house. Neither my husband nor I knew anything about construction. We prayed and studied. We searched many different types of houses and construction. We found a simple house that would fit our needs. Then we looked for materials. My father found a group of houses that were being destroyed. We borrowed a trailer and brought home all sorts of two by fours, and the likes, from these homes. We spent hours pulling out nails. A wood shed was built to house the boards. We then *searched for construction workers. We did not hire a builder. Each job required a new crew. This was hard and required a lot of research on our part because we did not know anything about construction. We did as much work as we could, digging the footings, roofing shingles, insulation, handling and finishing sheet rock, painting, etc. We only had a problem with one crew. The plumber had to be fired and removed when he showed up intoxicated. It took us about two years to build the house. The price of our house was a little over $20,000. The most awesome part of this gift is that we owe no money on our house or our property.*

We do not have a car payment, house payment or credit card payment to make each month. Recently we have built a studio to work in behind our home. My husband and I are both artists. Our dream is to work at home in our studio. We have a large garden. We are going to have chickens this spring. The wood shed is becoming a chicken coop.

*My point of sharing all of this is that some-
times God will provide in the most unlikely
ways. We had no idea that we would be able
to build what we did. I feel truly blessed my
husband had the wisdom to lead our family
in this direction. We have consecrated our
home and land to the Sacred Heart of Jesus
and the Immaculate Heart of Mary. Every
day we thank God for our home. We are truly grateful for the home and the conveniences
within it.*

*Over a year ago, we were listening to Radio
Wave on mej.com giving a first talk about
silver. We happened to have enough money
to purchase a 1000 ounce bar. The price at
the time was a little over 9.00 per ounce.**
*We purchased the bar the next week. We feel
truly blessed again.*

*God is good!!!!
Thank you for all that you do.*

C.L. Arkansas

---

* The price has since doubled in about a year's time. The 1000 ounce bar purchased
at $9,000 is presently worth $18,000, as of April 2010.

This family, living measured, is not an isolated case in reference to the past. Historically, it was the way man had always lived. But in this present time, it <u>is</u> an isolated case. This is Our Lady's wish: to reawaken in hearts the principles of Christianity that embraces living within the measure as God gives. With your sacrifices and efforts, working in collaboration with God, the fruit that will result is peace in seeing God meet all your needs. Most homes and the things in them and around them are the masters, enslaving those who 'think' they own the home or things, but rather the home or things own them. Do your home and things own you? Do you work for them, or do they work for you? Debt makes you work for 'them', you are their slave and your home and things are your master. You are constantly seeking money to pay the debt on your house instead of seeking boards to build it yourself. Instead of being your master, your home, your things, your money — all have a higher purpose which is to be used as Our Lady explains:

January 25, 2009

> **"...for all worldly things** (are) **to be a help for you to draw you closer to God the Creator..."**

"Worldly **things**" also include **money**. How can money be used to draw you and others closer to God? By returning 'things' back to their original intent that God ordained for them when He created them.

Jesus said you cannot serve two masters. You will "be devoted to one and despise the other". Do you realize what you just read? Did you hear it in your heart? Did you grasp the greatness of Jesus' words? You will be devoted to one and despise the other. Do not think this means you only have one or the other. In fact, many have two masters as opposed to one or the other. Most all people in this age of modernism have both masters. God and mammon. The world's enslavement through the economic, material disorder captures hundreds of millions through debt and consumerism. When you convert and become devoted to Jesus, a parallel takes place while you are still entangled to your devotion, being mastered by money, debt, home mortgage, car loans, etc. You suddenly realize you cannot free yourself from this god who dominates your life and who you suddenly begin to despise with disgust. Even if you are rich, money and your preoccupation with it dominate you. Not only nonbelievers need conversion but Christians especially need to convert and wake up to the fact, as a devotee of Christ,

you are serving two masters at the same time by being
devoted to one God and despising the other god. Ask
yourself as you convert or grow in conversion what do
you begin to despise? Now do you comprehend the
greatness of what this Scripture says? Do you hear
it in your heart? Many in the world today believe in
God, are devoted to Him but have indentured themselves as the servant of money/mammon. Our Lady's
words, Jesus' words are to free yourself from having
two masters. You must decide who you will serve. Our
Lady said this is a time of decision.

March 18, 1996

> **"...Decide, my children, it is the time of
> decision..."**

It's a time to decide for one master, that being God.

March 25, 1996

> **"...Do not let satan attract you through
> material things but, little children, decide
> for God who is freedom and love..."**

Once you realize you have to, with your whole heart,
completely become devoted to God it may take years
to undo in your heart what you have begun to despise.

It is why Our Lady said to give over to God all you possess rather than despise it. Get rid of the inordinate 'love' of money and/or things and come to serve the God you are devoted to.

The foundation set forth in the previous chapters gives the insights into what follows from here. Therefore, what you will read in the coming chapters may seem to be shifting away from the stories and miracles found in previous chapters. However, the following will allow you to come back to the previous chapters with greater understanding.

CHAPTER ELEVEN

God Made Silver and Gold

This brings us to the third revelation of 6/24, and it again ties to money and its use! But before revealing it, you, again, need to be more enlightened in order to understand the significance. Otherwise, the revelation will just pass right by you because the culture ruled by the current economic system has blinded us all, and in the case that follows, outright lied to us. As stated, along with the adorning of the Temple, the altars, and other holy objects, also in our present times, God ordained gold and silver as means of exchange for goods and services,. Historically, until about 1880, ounce for ounce, the price of gold was approximately 15 times that of silver, silver being priced less.[29] In other words, because, historically, the quantity of silver in the ground was approximately 15 times more than gold in the ground, gold was priced approximately 15 times higher than the price of silver, because gold is more rare.*

God made the two precious metals. But, compared side by side, silver is by far the more remarkable in what God designed into it. In that 'sense' alone, if silver was in shorter supply, it could conceivably rise up to be sold higher per ounce than gold! If the supply of silver traded places with gold, silver being 10 or 15 times less ounces available than gold, the price would naturally correct according to the supply and demand. Thereby, silver could be worth more than gold, because there would be less silver than gold. But can that actually happen? If silver continues to be used by man the way it is being used, it is not without a possibility.

Gold today is hovering around $1200 per ounce, as of April/May 2010.[30] If the price of silver were to correct to its historical price* in relation to gold, silver's price would be $80.00 per ounce — that is 15 times less than gold's price of $1200 because, as stated, histori-

---

* The historical ratios of below ground gold and silver cannot be known with complete certainty, but given the laws of supply and demand, a historical price ratio of approximately 15 times indicates a historical below ground ratio of approximately the same, 1880 and prior. As civilization progressed moving into the 1900s, and as the market became more global, more factors aside from supply and demand entered the precious metals markets, and the price ratio between gold and silver strayed from its historical precedent. Today this ratio is much greater than 15 (silver) to one (gold). As of the date of this writing, March/May 2010, the ratio is approximately 65 (silver) to 1 (gold). It appears the price ratio is ripe for a correction.

cally, there is 15 times less gold than silver in the earth. However, reserve estimates from the United States Geological Survey indicate that, currently, underground silver reserves may even be as little as 8.5 times that of underground gold reserves, meaning that silver could be priced even higher at around $141.00 per ounce.[31] Gold and silver are both precious metals. For the most part, the supply and demand historically determines the price through the laws of measurement — usage — supply and demand that are programmed into creation. Man can manipulate it, suppress it, cheat on the scales of weight and measurement but sooner or later the natural law of nature, programmed into creation, will cause self-correction through supply and demand through the need and uses by man.

Virtually all the gold that has ever been mined, about 5.2 billion ounces,[32] is still around.[33] In regard to silver, approximately 47.9 billion ounces of silver have been mined throughout history.[34] Of that, the exact percentage is not known, as estimates amongst experts vary, but it appears that a good portion, maybe even roughly half[35] of the 47.9 billion ounces of silver that have been mined throughout history have been consumed in industrial applications and will not ever be recovered. That silver cannot be recovered and used again for some other purpose. In recent years, thousands of industrial applications have been using up about 45–50% of the world's annual silver production.[36] Given the increasing number of unrecoverable silver applications in all fields, it appears that a goodly amount of the 45–50% of silver will continue to be used up in various industrial and related applications in the future. Shockingly, aside from industry, coins, jewelry, and individual private stocks (i.e. silver that is already being used), at present there are only approximately 771 million ounces of known reserves of above ground silver bullion available to potential purchasers.[37] Bullion refers to silver held in the form of bars or other convenient shapes that has not yet been made into coins, jewelry, etc., or used in industry.

What about what is still below ground? According to the U.S. Government's 'U'nited 'S'tates 'G'eological 'S'urvey, or the USGS 2010 Report, the estimated world supply for silver still in the earth is 400,000 metric tons.[38] Yearly worldwide mine production,* the survey shows, is 21,400 metric tons.[39] That means if mine production continues at the present rate of 21,400 metric tons per year, the world's below ground estimated supply of 400,000 metric tons could be depleted in about 18½

---

* Here, mine production refers to the amount of silver mined from the earth and brought up to the surface.

years! Silver, a miracle metal from God, could possibly be the only metal in the periodic table of elements that has been essentially mined out of the earth (excluding small pockets of silver that are not feasibly mined). In addition, with industry using it in products for consumers, as well as other unrecoverable industrial applications, a goodly portion of above ground silver is, for the most part, gone forever. When you look at the fact that 45% of mined silver today is being used in industrial and consumable application, take into consideration that a fair amount of that 45% is used in a way that the silver is non-retrievable. You then can 'read the signs' which suggest a scenario that even above ground silver is also being depleted, never to circulate again! An unhealthy portion of above ground silver is literally used for one time applications and will no longer exist in a reusable state. This course is set if the path of consumption stays its course.

However, the 18½ year time table derived from the USGS is the survey's statistical estimate and does not account for the rapid growing industrial consumption of such countries as China and India, nor does it take into account new discoveries for silver's use and applications not yet applied. Some experts say world supply could be depleted in as little as 14 years.[40] No one can say for certain because many factors could slow consumption down, such as the continual economic down turn, although technology is growing exponentially. However, the fact that silver is being consumed more than ever before and is less in supply than gold above ground is a cause to use common sense and to discern the signs of the time. Our Lady often says to use well this time of grace God gives. Though the world is often blind to these things, those who are the salt of the earth are afforded the grace to see. It is stated in *Why Silver? Why Now?*:

> *"If you look back over a decade or so what you find is industrial demand is around 35% of the total silver market. Today the industrial demand is around 45% of the silver demand. And what that means is that it's the fastest growing segment and it's the most important segment from the standpoint of most of the applications in industrial are not retrievable economically to get the silver back out."*[41]

In 2009, the United Nations 'I'nternational 'T'elecommunications 'U'nion, or abbreviated as the ITU, Report showed the world had hit the 4.1 billion mark for cell phones. Four billion cell phones! Because of technology advancing so quickly, most by now are buried in the garbage, dumped across the earth. Cell phones are just one of thousands of products which use and consume silver that can never be retrieved.

But not to worry, the government has hordes of silver. Does the U.S. Government really have huge stockpiles of silver? In *Why Silver? Why Now?*, it is stated:

"In the case of silver as more and more industrial applications are being discovered, silver mining has been insufficient to meet yearly demand for 16 straight years. This fact alone bears close scrutiny, as this silver production deficit is unprecedented in history.

"There's been more demand for silver than there has been new supply from the mines for 20 years. The government has been filling that gap. The metals are running out. The demand is not going to go down because it's needed for so many things.

"Supply and demand of any commodity have to equal — they do. And we've had a deficit in silver for 16 consecutive years from 1990 to 2005. And the way that that deficit, that I'll define for you, has been met is through above ground supplies, and the deficit simply means that the amount of silver that is mined from all mining activity has not

met that annual demand. So the point, to make it very clear: in 1990, 'x' amount of silver was mined, but 'x plus' an amount was needed. And that happened every year for 16 straight years that the amount mined did not match the amount demanded by the marketplace. The supply and demand did equal because the above ground stock pile has been eaten away again and again and again. So now again, the supply side is not meeting the demand so the squeeze in the silver prices has started to take effect already and I believe it will accelerate in the future."[42]

The government's stockpile, its resource for the security of its citizens, is gone? Gone! The U.S. Government is now a buyer at current worldwide prices. The U.S. Government sold off its reserve to make up the deficit for 16 years. According to the year 2010 Silver Mineral Commodities Summaries, produced by United States Geological Survey, it lists:

"GOVERNMENT STOCKPILE: NONE"

It is a surprise to many that the U.S. Government has no reserves! But what has all this got to do with the third revelation of 6/24? Yet, still more must be explained so as to comprehend the significance.

CHAPTER TWELVE

Man Cannot Duplicate It

Silver is like a miracle. Its characteristics have the fingerprint of God upon it. It reflects back to you your own image perfectly just as if you were looking into a mirror. The moon, lighting up the earth at night, actually has no light of its own but reflects the light of the 'sun,' and in doing so, lights up the dark earth. This reality of nature reveals a creation revelation that parallels a spiritual reality of Our Lady lighting up the darkness by reflecting the love of Her 'Son' Jesus. It is stated in Revelation Chapter 12:

"A woman clothed with the sun, with the moon under Her feet."

Our Lady said God wants to speak to you.

March 25, 1990

"...God wants to save you and sends you messages through men, nature, and so many things ..."

The moon is without light, but when man looks up upon a moon lighting up the night and can see his way through the darkness, it is because the moon is clothed with the sun. The reflection of the light is why man, for centuries, has referred to 'the light' of the moon, "by the light of the **'silvery'** moon." Man used the word 'silvery' for the moon because of silver's reflectiveness. Silver is not only known for this remarkable trait of reflecting light and mirroring an image through light, but also for healing. Our Lady has come to heal the world. She has repeatedly referred us to God the Creator and His creation to discover remedies to heal both the body and the soul of man. Silver is an example of this. Our Creator programmed into silver an ongoing miracle that is amazing, but equally amazing is that it is a miracle that man has discarded.

Greece, Rome and other ancient civilizations used silver to stop infection. Hippocrates, as the Father of Medicine, healed wounds with silver. But some are told silver can damage the body. Swiss alchemist, Theophratus Von Hohenheim, the Father of Toxicology, who lived in the 16th century, used silver as medicine, along with other elements of the earth. He said:

"All things are poison and nothing is without poison; only the 'dose' makes that thing a poison or not."[43]

Silver's history is well known and only now is coming of age in our time. What today's highly advanced man does not know, ancient man did know. Man was using silver for healing and sanitizing for millenniums, from lining water containers with silver to prevent contamination to placing silver coins in water and milk to prevent spoilage. The anti-bacterial property of silver would certainly seem miraculous through the ages, before the microscope. But even today its miracle-like quality, programmed into its creation, can do what man cannot. The staph germ in hospitals, known as the 'superbug,' is called such because it has repeatedly built up resistance to what man can do to control it. Silver simply kills the germ. The amazing thing, while man tries and retries to create a product that kills it, the germ does the same in building resistance continuing to thrive, both sides upping the ante at each stage. Silver, by the hand of God, works in a way unchanging since the dawn of creation, and man cannot duplicate it with his pharmaceutical and chemical creations. The Silver Institute states:

"Silver's anti-bacterial powers have been tested and proven scientifically even though its power as a bactericide has been known for centuries. The ancient Phoenicians, for example, knew that water, wine, or vinegar kept in silver vessels stayed fresh during long sea voyages.

"Only recently, however, have scientists discovered how the white metal does its work. Quite simply, silver interrupts a bacteria cell's ability to form chemical bonds essential to its survival. These bonds produce the cell's physical structure so bacteria in the presence of silver literally falls apart. Cells in humans and other animals have thick walls and are not disturbed by silver. Therefore, silver prevents bacteria growth but is harmless to humans."[44]

Lucian Lucia, professor of Chemistry at North Carolina State University, says:

"Nano-particles of silver detected in the cell wall of microbe bacteria cannot build up resistance to silver, as they can to antibiotics because of the way the silver attacks, destroying the structure of the cells and killing them. Antibiotics, on the other hand, suppress the activity of bacteria but

*does not necessarily kill them. That is the beauty
of silver. There is no way to develop a resistance
to it.* "[45]

The Silver Institute states:

*"One of the most important uses of silver as
a biocide is in hospitals and other health care
facilities because they grapple with a type of
life-threatening Staph germ, referred to as a
'superbug' which is resistant to almost all chemical antibiotics, so many hospitals are employing
silver-imbedded equipment including surgical
tools, catheters, needles, stethoscopes, furniture,
door handles and even paper files."* [46]

Why is it that in this modern time of high technology
something so basic is just now coming of age? Dr. Al-
lan Spreen notes, in regards to the natural antibacterial
property contained in silver:

*"We hear little about them because of the fact
that they are not patentable and, therefore, have
no profit potential, at least nowhere near the level
pharmaceutical companies desire."* [47]

The Silver Institute also states:

"One of the most promising applications is in silver-imbedded bandages for burns and wound victims. The silver ions help prevent infection but also speed healing because the body doesn't have to focus its energy on fighting infection.

"Currently we're seeing a surge of applications for silver-based biocides in all areas: industrial, commercial and consumer. New products are being introduced almost daily. Established companies are incorporating silver based products in current lines — clothing, refrigerators, mobile phones, computers, washing machines, vacuum cleaners, keyboards, countertops, furniture handles and more. The newest trend is the use of nano-silver particles to deliver silver ions."[48]

"Industrial demand for silver has grown consistently for the past three decades because of silver's many unique properties, including its strength, malleability, and ductility...its unparalleled electrical and thermal conductivity...its sensitivity to and high reflectance of light...and its ability to endure extreme temperature ranges."[49]

If you had a shovel, its use would most likely stay
with a small circle of users: you, your family members,
and at most, a neighbor who may borrow it — no more
than a few people. How about your vacuum cleaner?
How many different people use it? Three or four people? What about the food you eat? How many hands
does it go through? Four-five-ten? 'Think' through
much of civilization's history of how unsanitary man
lived through lack of readily available water, soap, etc.
A man working in his barn, shoveling manure, con-
taminates his shovel. But it is limited who comes into
contact with the shovel. Man to man contact is limited
by the nature of its use. But one thing is in contact
with everyone, whether it was handled after someone
handled the garbage, animals, or whether one went to
the bathroom or was sick. Contact with this thing is
made with nearly everything of every sort on the earth.
It is nasty.

In this modern time, with so much talk of germs
and sanitation, moms would say after handling it, always wash your hands. What is it? Money! It is nasty,
no matter how clean you are or how clean money
looks. Unlike a shovel or any other thing, money
flows throughout civilization from one man to another.
Man's special attention of money keeps him from rare-

ly losing it, and so it passes through a myriad of people.
From the clean suit and tie man, to the street vendor,
to the garbage man, to the beggar, to the grocery store
clerk, to the jewelry store owners, to society's most
degraded and filthiest: all handle the same money. Its
reputation, especially before modern sanitation, for the
most part, was unknown with the possibility of being
covered with germs. There is no other physical object
that passes so quickly through so many, that travels
so far, from the richest to the poorest, from the clean-
est to the filthiest, than money. That is why it is said
of money: 'In circulation.' It circulates, temporarily
owned by so many different owners. It thrives under
the protection of these 'bodyguards' as it is handed
from one guard to another. You don't want to touch
the bathroom door handle when you come out of public bathrooms. Yet, we all take money as exchange
from the one who just came out of the bathroom, who
didn't wash, who touched the handle and who gives
out of his hand your change.

It is a comfort to know God had all this figured out.
Silver's miraculous power from God prevents it from
being a host for the transmission of germs. This cannot
be without God's design. Knowing this one precious
metal would be used by so many, even above gold,

from the rich to the poor, throughout history, God must have built into silver traits that maintain purity, even though it passes through hands that are impure in the physical realm.

CHAPTER THIRTEEN

Former Generations Would Die Laughing

While medical use of silver, and silver's use as a germ free exchange, serves man, we still must grapple with a tremendous growth market of silver consumption. As more avenues in industry apply silver in their products, the shorter the supply becomes. On top of that, the frivolous waste of silver in TV's, cell phones, electronic games, and thousands of other electronic uses are literally eating this silver away forever, thereby making this metal more rare. All the while, on a daily basis, new uses and products are brought into the consumer market, as well as new discoveries of its application for industry. The precious metal is daily becoming more precious. In essence, man does not know how precious the true value of silver really is.

Now that you understand the miracles of silver, how man is destroying a portion of it through consumerism, and how Our Lady identifies that due to the spirit of

'consumerism,'* we do not know 'true value', we can
now begin to understand the lie which helps us to iden-
tify what is of value both physically and spiritually. By
educating yourself and discovering the value and use of
silver for means to preserve or sustain yourselves and
in some cases, for the exchange of goods and services,
as it has always been in history, you can begin to see the
lie. This brings us to the significance of the 3rd revelation
of 6/24 and as with Matthew 6:24, it is, very remarkably,
tied to money.

In 5000 years of history, **never** has a paper currency
survived longer than about 50 years. R. S. News reports:

*"Since the advent of the world's most powerful
central bank, the Federal Reserve, the West has
seen two Great Unravelings — the Depression of
the 1930s and the Financial Crisis of the 2000's.
This works out to one definitive unraveling every
50 years, or once every two-to-three generations."*[50]

But in recalling what was written earlier in this writing,
you may respond that Byzantine's economy lasted 800
years. Yes, but remember it was backed by the measurement of gold. For decades the dollar was the standard

---

* **"...In this time, when due to the spirit of consumerism, one forgets what it means
to love and to cherish true values, I invite you again, little children, to put God in
the first place in your life. Do not let satan attract you through material things..."**
March 25, 1996

for all world currencies. Oil was priced in dollars and the whole world's confidence was in the dollar. The dollar was strong when it stood with truth. "In God We Trust" written on the dollar meant something because the measurement of its worth was backed by what God created and ordained for it: a precious metal, silver, in which the wisdom of man made the dollar to depend on.

The United States, being a Christian nation, added to the might of the dollar. When you held a dollar, you held a certificate for that amount in silver, redeemable in that amount of silver coins. The dollar was not just paper, it was a certification of silver, awarded to you upon demand, and known as a silver certificate. This is stability and security. But, this, of course, restricts man's economy from expanding beyond the bounds of the silver which backs up each dollar. Man, in his lust for an expanding economy beyond the measurement God programmed for him, broke those bonds. A spirit of consumerism and materialism broke loose upon the nation and thereby, upon the whole world. It inevitably will collapse when the illusion becomes fully understood. Because of this, man will pay a bitter price. A worldwide integrated economy developed beyond Heaven's prescribed bounds. A system driven along by satan is dangerous to man, both spiritually and physically, because this economy was built on a lie in order to expand more than the limited 'silver' backed dollar economy would allow. The real worth, the 'real value' of a dollar came to an end for all those who held the dollar known as a silver certificate. This happened through an order from the government in league with the financial banks of the central bank, known as the Federal Reserve, a non-government entity.

It was a plan schemed, a calculated 'creeping gradualism,' to get unsuspecting citizens into accepting the lie, to pass it by the people without their notice. <u>And the revelation is the day it happened</u>. **6/24**…that would be **June 24, 1968**.[51] This was the date chosen that, hence forth, silver backing the dollar could no longer be redeemed. In its place, on **6/24**, man produced the lie, slipping away a certificate of silver to sneak in a piece of paper, backed now by nothing, called a Federal Reserve Note. The Federal Reserve* is a deceptive name given to an entity that is not part of the Federal Government, but rather a private system ran by the central bank. Again, the Federal Reserve is not connected to the Federal Government, but a banking system ran by banking people, serving their own interests. With silver no longer backing the dollar, the dollar began on an

---

*   One of 12 banks set up under the Federal Reserve system to hold reserves and discount commercial paper for affiliated banks in their respective districts.

accelerated path to becoming worth less and less. The exchange that took place on 6/24 in which the true value of the silver certificate was replaced for a faith belief in the false value of a Federal Reserve Note slipped by without the masses comprehending what was happening. The exchange was giving up something of worth, 'silver certificates,' for something without worth. On

The top dollar is the one dollar silver certificate, backed by and could be exchanged for silver. The second dollar is the non-government Federal Reserve Note, backed by nothing of any value whatsoever. When paper is printed and has no worth, it is called fiat money.

the paper dollar bill, the words 'silver certificate' were removed and replaced with the words 'Federal Reserve Note.' With silver no longer backing the dollar, the value of the dollar now was only the people's 'historical faith' in it, the memory held in remembrance that the dollar once had worth, not comprehending that with the exchange made from the silver certificate to the Federal Reserve Note, the dollar's present worth was –0– in intrinsic value. The plan put forth in the 1930s by the schemes of the banking advisors was so dangerous that even in Thomas Jefferson's day, his foresighted wisdom is shown in a letter to John Taylor in 1816:

> *"And I sincerely believe, with you, that banking establishments are more dangerous than standing armies."*[52]

Jefferson saw what would destroy a nation more so than a standing army! Jefferson was not alone in his fore-sight. Abraham Lincoln once said in November 1864:

> *"The money power preys upon the nation in times of peace, and conspires against it in times of adversity. It is more despotic than monarchy, more insolent than autocracy, more selfish than bureaucracy. It denounces as public enemies, all who question its methods or throw light upon its*

*crimes. I have two great enemies, the Southern
Army in front of me, and the financial institutions
in the rear. Of the two, the one in my rear is my
greatest foe."*[53]

Yet, no one sees what is happening today that Jefferson
foresaw 250 years ago.

Exchanging the words *silver certificate* with words,
Federal Reserve Note, which again happened through
the Federal Reserve, which is <u>not</u> the government, could
never have happened several decades before 6/24/68.
People were too smart, they had common sense and
would never have accepted something that looks like
paper, feels like paper, and is paper, and call it money.
They would have died laughing and would have viewed
anyone who would accept paper, and call it money, as
nothing but a fool. To accept this fake money, man had
to be conditioned, dumbed down to lose common sense,
to lose confidence in God's ways, and in turn, to lose
wisdom. G.K. Chesterton said:

"'The first effect of not believing in God, is that
you lose your common sense.' *Since the line
never gets quoted correctly, let's quote it correctly
again:* 'The first effect of not believing in God, is
that you lose your common sense.' *That means*

*that in order for us to recover our common sense,
we have to recover our faith. In order for us to
recover our faith, we need religious renewal and
reform."*[54]

Indeed, man today, has lost common sense because
society does not place God in the first place. How else
can it be explained that man accepted to exchange a
certificate that paid silver on demand with an imposter
look-a-like certificate, a Federal Reserve Note, that paid
nothing on demand? As a magician with a fast hand,
6/24/68 took place with little or no resistance. Man,
during that time, was too mesmerized by the age of the
hula hoop and the likes of what followed to even notice. Thirty years before **6/24**/68, any man on the street
would have called this action illegal and counterfeiting,
even traitorous. Common sense mentality could not
have reconciled the lie of buying something or paying
for services with something that has no value. Everyone
trusted the silver dollar certificate because they knew
if they wanted silver they had the confidence that when
they went into a bank, <u>anywhere</u>, they would come out
with silver. Silver dimes, silver quarters, silver dollars.
The irony in discovering this lie is that you can take advantage of what men of another age would call this age,
a bunch of fools. By not being a fool, you can presently

take worthless fiat paper dollars* and buy as much silver as you can before everyone else who are fools wake up. In other words, today you can take advantage of this foolish age by getting *free silver* by exchanging worthless paper for it. If this was not so serious, it would be funny. Indeed, man, in the first half of the 1900s, would be laughing and talking about that on every street corner. But the opportunity to get 'free silver' will go away as more people 'unfool' themselves and learn of truth and God's ways. What is really funny is that you can actually buy silver today with dollars that are no different than the fake money found in a Monopoly game, except instead of a game, you can actually use worthless fiat money to buy silver. How long will this last? When enough people, all who have been fooled, are no longer fooled because they acquired common sense. Our Lady tells us Jesus is:

December 2, 2007

"...the light of common sense."

But when everyone wakes up to the light of common sense, it will be too late. When that happens, no one will give you silver for fiat dollars.

---

* Paper money backed by nothing of value.

CHAPTER FOURTEEN

The Virtue of Delayed Gratification.
The Danger of Immediate Gratification
And Usury

What if a man walked up to you and said he would loan you one hundred thousand dollars 240 different times so that he could collect all his interest each month on what you borrowed? Then he told you these 240 different loans would make him a lot of money, $100,744.98 to be precise, on top of the $100,000 you must pay him back, a total of which would be $200,744.98. Would you answer, "Do you think I'm a fool?" or would you die laughing? Or would you do both?

The dollar, on 6/24, lost all of its intrinsic value or, you might say, lost its <u>true</u> value and all for the sake of 'love of money,' the root of all evil. You cannot serve two masters, God and money. Silver, God's creation, was divorced from the dollar, and paper, man's creation, was married to the private Federal Reserve. The dollar, at that point became a lie, a false image projecting something it was not, a deception by the central bank to build and expand the economy, lending enormous amounts of paper notes that were supplied by a printing press. All this was done to tempt people with consumerism, by the banking system, to go in debt for the immediate gratification materialism offers, a lie many are beginning to be able to see, as now they are enslaved by it, just as Our Lady said:

June 25, 1989

"...the world and material goods lead you into slavery. satan is active in this plan..."

Former generations would not borrow, rather they believed in delayed gratification, sacrifice, and paying for what they acquired. Financial advisor, Dave Ramsey, tells the following story that illustrates this point:

"Since the Civil War, we have seen a steady change in the way we Americans handle our money. As a boy in the 1850s, prior to the Civil War, my great, great grandfather lived in Indiana. In his memoirs he mentions a family who owned a neighboring farm. This family got the fever to move West but couldn't because unlike most anyone else in the country, they owed money on their farm. The language he used to discuss this mortgage gave

insight into the attitude of the day regarding debt.
He gave the impression that one should pity this
family as if they had cancer or view them as sin-
ners who had some skeleton in their closet. This
view of debt is completely foreign to us today.
Astonishingly the mortgage in question was only
$5. The generation of people who set up house-
keeping in the 1930s and the 1940s was scarred by
the Great Depression. Those folks would borrow
very seldom and they lived under their means.
They would be shocked by the way most families
live today.[55]

The present age of immediate gratification in which it
is common practice to 'borrow' from your future so to
enjoy today, is unbiblical and consequently will lead
to slavery. In reality, to borrow to satisfy immediate
gratification is stealing from yourself money that you do
not have, have not yet earned, and have no guarantee
you will earn. No Biblical principle supports this. The
present system of usury will cause the present economic
system's suicide. That is the judgement sentence of
God. You can call it a correction or a return to the
correct price value, which always happens in a self-
correction, but in the end, it is God's judgement of
natural law programmed into creation for everything.

Man cannot escape this corrective judgement, in this case, the sentence for the sin of usury. Specifically, what is usury? In the book titled, <u>The Creature From Jekyll Island</u>, G. Edward Griffin writes:

> "Centuries ago, *usury* was defined as any interest charged for a loan. Modern usage has redefined it as *excessive* interest. Certainly, any amount of interest charged for a *pretended* loan is excessive. The dictionary, therefore, needs a new definition. *Usury: The charging of any interest on a loan of fiat money.**
>
> "Let us, therefore, look at debt and interest in this light. **Thomas Edison** summed up the immorality of the system when he said:
>
>> 'People who will not turn a shovel full of dirt on the project nor contribute a pound of materials will collect more money...than will be people who will supply all the materials and do all the work.'[56]

---

* A Friend of Medjugorje does not advocate borrowing. The text used here is Griffin's and he is correct in what is stated, in regards to 'pretended loans,' meaning money one loans of which is not earned by you. But, a Friend of Medjugorje states money that is also earned and lent as time value/compounded is also usury and sinful.

Griffin continues:

"Is that an exaggeration? Let us consider the purchase of a $100,000 home in which $30,000 repre-
sents the cost of the land, architect's fee, sales commissions, building permits, and that sort of thing and
$70,000 is the cost of labor and building materials. If
the home buyer puts up $30,000 as a down payment,
then $70,000 must be borrowed. If the loan is issued
at 11%* over a 30-year period, the amount of interest paid will be $167,806. That means the amount
paid to those who lend the money is about 2 ½ times
greater than paid to those who provide all the labor
and all the materials. It is true that this figure repre-
sents the time-value of that money over thirty years
and easily could be justified on the basis that a lender
deserves to be compensated for surrendering the use
of his capital for half a lifetime. But that assumes the
lender actually had something to surrender, that he
had earned the capital, saved it, and then lent it for
construction of someone else's house. What are we
to think, however, about a lender who did nothing to
earn the money, had not saved it, and, in fact, simply
created it out of thin air? What is the time-value of
nothing?[57]

---

* Some may look at this 11% rate as being a high example, but mortgage interest
rates have risen as high as 16 plus percent in the past 35 years.

Continuing on in <u>The Creature of Jekyll Island</u>, Griffin states:

> "...every dollar that exists today, either in the form
> of currency, checkbook money, or even credit card
> money — in other words, our *entire* money supply
> — exists only because it was borrowed by someone;
> perhaps not you, but *someone*. That means all the
> American dollars in the entire world are earning dai-
> ly and compounded interest for the banks which cre-
> ated them. A portion of every business venture, every
> investment, every profit, every transaction which in-
> volves money — and that even includes *losses* and the
> payment of *taxes* — a portion of all that is earmarked
> as payment to a bank. And what did the banks do
> to earn this perpetually flowing river of wealth? Did
> they lend out their own capital obtained through the
> investment of stockholders? Did they lend out the
> hard-earned savings of their depositors? No, neither
> of these was their major source of income. They sim-
> ply waved the magic wand called fiat money."[58]

What Griffin shows, by the flow of such unearned
wealth under the guise of interest, can only be viewed
as usury of the highest magnitude. He says, "*It is the supreme instrument of usury.*" But let's take another view
for an example: What if you loaned money that was not
yours? Say someone gives you $100,000 to hold until

they come back from overseas ten years from now. You realize what they gave you to safeguard, you can loan it to someone at 8% interest compounded yearly over ten years. If the person makes equal, annual payments on the loan, the total amount of interest collected from the loan at the end of the 10 years would be approximately $49,000 that you made. Is this just? No, it is sin in two ways. First, it is usury and second, the gain is not yours because you did not earn the money that was loaned.

This is what the banks do. How do the banks loan money which is not theirs? Again, Griffin writes:

> "It is a form of modern serfdom in which the great mass of society works as indentured servants to a ruling class of financial nobility.

> "The entire function of this machine is to convert debt into money. It's just that simple. First, the Fed [Federal Reserve Bank] takes all the government bonds which the public does not buy and writes a check to Congress in exchange for them. (It acquires other debt obligations as well, but government bonds comprise most of its inventory.) **There is no money to back up this check. These fiat dollars are created on the spot for that purpose.** By calling those bonds 'reserves,' the Fed then uses them as the base for cre-

ating nine additional dollars for every dollar created for the bonds themselves! The money created for the bonds is spent by the government, whereas the money created on top of those bonds is the source of all the bank loans made to the nation's businesses and individuals. The result of this process is the same as creating money on a printing press, but the illusion is based on an accounting trick rather than a printing trick. The bottom line is that Congress and the banking cartel has the privilege of collecting interest on money which it creates out of nothing, a perpetual override on every American dollar that exists in the world. Congress, on the other hand, has access to unlimited funding without having to tell the voters their taxes are being raised through the process of inflation. If you understand this paragraph, you understand the Federal Reserve System." [59]

If you do not understand this previous part of Chapter 14, further examples will make it clearer and then, perhaps, you may want to reread what Griffin stated in the last 2 or 3 pages. Do additional research, if necessary, so to grasp it. Your understanding of this whole chapter is crucial to your future and your decisions.

If usury is a sin, why does the Church not denounce it throughout the world? Pope Paul VI said:

"From some fissure* the smoke of satan has entered the temple of God."[60]

What has happened to the Church? We have even our parishes borrowing money to build churches at unquestionable rates of interest to pay back. All this has happened even though the Church once condemned usury through several ecclesiastical councils. Bishops in historic succession, in general councils of the Church, repeatedly condemned usury. How can this be reconciled as acceptable today and yet so clearly condemned since the Church Fathers repeatedly condemned such? Has the Church collaborated with usury? Is this part of the smoke that has entered the Church that Pope Paul VI spoke of? There are historians who believe the weakening of priests' convictions against usury is the primary reason for usury becoming acceptable, even more than any theological reason brought forth! Fr. Pete Scott, past rector of the Holy Cross Seminary in Australia, wrote in 2005:

"The early Fathers of the Church protested against usury in the strongest terms and numerous ecclesiastical decrees in the 12th and 13th centuries

---

* The common translation says, "The smoke of satan has entered the Church." But Pope Paul VI said it in Italian: *"Da qualche fessura sia entrato il fumo di satana nel tempio di Dio,"* which translates, *"From some fissure the smoke of satan has entered the temple of God."* Fissure means: "A narrow opening or crack of considerable length and depth usually occurring from some breaking or parting; crack, divide."

enforced its prohibition under pain of excommunication and denial of Catholic burial. There has been, however, a relaxation of the Church's law on the subject, since the development of Protestantism made it socially acceptable, and in the 19th century made it an inescapable reality of daily life."[61]

It was John Calvin who broke Holy tradition for cultural accommodation. The Catholic Church followed, coming to the same conclusion, and eventually relaxed Church law through the 1917 Code of Canon Law, Canon 1543:

"If a commodity which is consumed by its first use be lent on the stipulation that it becomes the property of the borrower, who is bound to return to the lender not the thing itself, but its equivalent only, the lender may not receive any payment by reason of the loan itself. In the giving or lending of such a commodity, however, it is not in itself unlawful to make an arrangement for the recovery of interest at the rate allowed by the civil law, unless that rate is clearly excessive..."[62]

But where is the interest not excessive? Look at any car, land, home, etc., amortization schedule loan payment, and you will see something is very wrong. All interest is collected first, little or no principal is paid up front against the loan debt pay back, and by the time you pay off the loan, you may have paid double and even triple the amount of the original loan. Can you honestly ask in your heart: Is this not what Scripture and the Church Fathers condemned? The smoke of satan has entered God's temple through a crack and our pulpits are silenced by participating in usury!

In Summa Theologica (lla llae Q.78, A.1), written between 1265–1274, Thomas Aquinas writes:

> *"He commits an injustice who sells wine or wheat and who asks for double payment, i.e., one, the return of the thing in equal measure, the other the price of the 'use', which is called usury...Now money, according to the Philosopher Aristotle was invented chiefly for the purpose of exchange; and consequently the chief and principal purpose of money is its consumption or alienation whereby it is sunk in exchange. Hence it is by its very nature unlawful to take payment for the use of money lent, which payment is known as usury: and just as man is bound to restore other ill-gotten goods, so is he obliged to restore the money which he has taken in usury."[63]*

Fr. Walter Farrell, O.P. wrote in 1940:

> *"Wherever usury is found it is wrong; and its evil*
> *is manifest. It is absurdly simple to understand*
> *that to charge a man twice for the same thing is al-*
> *ways unjust; yet that is precisely what usury does,*
> *it sells the same thing twice. The trick is possible*
> *only when the thing sold or loaned is consumed*
> *in its very first use, things like wine or sandwiches,*
> *or money. When we demand, over and above the*
> *return of the original sum of money loaned, an*
> *added amount for the use of the money, our act is*
> *the same as selling a man a glass of wine and then*
> *charging him for the privilege of drinking it."*[64]

Our Lady has come to make us see how dumbed down we have become. No power to discern. Our Lady says:

May 2, 2009

> **"...You are permitting sin to overcome you more**
> **and more. You are permitting it to master you and**
> **to take away your power of discernment..."**

Usury was resoundingly denounced throughout Church history and now, because of cultural accommodation, the people want it — the Church does also. What dangers did the early Church Fathers see with usury that they prohibited its use *"under the pain of excommunication and denial of a Catholic burial?"* Most all of us would agree and say that is way too harsh of a penalty, but today we have gone to the complete other side of the pendulum of excommunication, etc., with a total embracing of usury even within the Church. But the early Church Fathers were able to understand through their life of prayer and self-denial, that unbridled usury would lead to the destruction of entire societies and civilizations. Modernism works to sanitize what was always filthy, making it appear to be clean and disguised as light. Yet Our Lady says:

May 25, 2010

"...satan, too, does not sleep and through modernism diverts you and leads you to his way..."

We have a bailout mentality throughout the culture, as well as throughout the Church. The mentality, 'money is the fix,' is invading the Church like smoke through an encroachment of a 'creeping gradualism.' It invades God's temple, just as smoke goes not through the doors, but under the crack without having to open the door. And nobody's eyes are burned by the smoke enough to realize there is a fire in their midst. Our Lady is call-

ing the Church to wake up. Quit following the culture.
Drive out the smoke of satan. Lead the culture! Fr. Peter Scott writes:

> *"The reason for this change or apparent change
> in the Church's attitude towards usury is that
> in modern times, owing to the organization of
> economic life, money has practically become
> a form of capital, and the Church follows her
> traditional policy in regulating her attitude
> towards it. As usual she temporarily adjusts her
> discipline as far as possible to the needs of the
> age, even when these needs are the result of a state
> of things **of which she does not approve**, and
> allows the faithful to act in accordance with social
> customs sanctioned by existing civil law, provided
> these customs are not manifestly immoral or
> unjust."* [65]

But when is it just? That is the point! It is not moral
nor just. Remember Thomas Aquinas said:

> *"…it is by its very nature unlawful to take pay-
> ment for the use of money lent…"* [66]

Remember also Our Lady said on May 25, 2010:

"...satan...through modernism diverts you and leads you to his way..."

These above two things are to be remembered to tell us that modernism's approach to money becoming a commodity that is sold, as if it were corn or oil, is "unlawful by its very nature." Aristotle said money *" was invented chiefly for the purpose of exchange."* Through the method of usury, satan now diverts and leads us the wrong way. We've accepted the lie of usury that money is a commodity or a 'time value' product. This is also contradicted by Thomas Aquinas when he echoed Aristotle, writing:

> *"The chief and principle purpose of money is its consumption or alienation whereby it is sunk in exchange."*[67]

Remember Fr. Scott's words that She, **the Church, "does not approve of,"** but allows social customs of existing civil law, provided these customs are not manifestly immoral or unjust. But is the Church asleep to what is happening, even to a church loan through usury? Our Lady said:

February 25, 2000

"...Wake up from the sleep of unbelief and sin..."

Many are asleep, but these words can awaken you to the immorality of usury, just as Thomas Edison said:

> *"People who will not turn a shovel full of dirt on the project nor contribute a pound of materials will collect more money...than will be people who will supply all the materials and do all the work."*[68]

But Edison is speaking about those who do the work on the house and how much greater the lender will collect than they who labor to build it. But what about the one who buys and labors to earn money that must pay through a mortgage all the extra money for the building and construction? More money than will be people who were paid to supply all the materials and do all the work couple the interest and the buyer pays twice: to those who build and to those who loan?"

How can anyone say the following amortization is not the fullness of usury that the Church continually and repeatedly condemned? The average mortgage rate on a 30-year fixed rate mortgage loan from 1985 to 2010, a 25 year period, is 8.2%.[69] So, let's say 'you' get a mortgage at 8% as the following illustrates:

Mortgage Loan Amount $100,000.00
Interest Rate   8% compounded monthly
Pay Back   20 years monthly payments

The following is a schedule showing the payback of principal (the amount of money you actually borrowed) and interest (what you owe the bank for borrowing the principal), called an Amortization Schedule. Study every detail minutely. Think about what you are looking at. Don't worry about being intimidated at first. It will easily become clear. The more time you study the amortization schedule, and the breakdown of your loan, the more you will see why the system now has a judgment against itself by God, just as Jesus did against the money changers in the temple. Do not move on in this book until you have thoroughly and prayerfully examined this payment schedule, and read and study the yellow highlighted points. By doing so the rest of what you read in the book becomes much more understandable and clear.

20 Year $100,000.00 Loan Amortization Schedule
Monthly Payments

Example of first five months of year 1

Payment No.	Due Date	Payment	Interest	Principal	Balance
1	Jan, 2011	$ 836.44	$ 666.67	$ 169.77	$ 99,830.23
2	Feb, 2011	$ 836.44	$ 665.53	$ 170.91	$ 99,659.32
3	Mar, 2011	$ 836.44	$ 664.40	$ 172.04	$ 99,487.28
4	Apr, 2011	$ 836.44	$ 663.26	$ 173.19	$ 99,314.09
5	May, 2011	$ 836.44	$ 662.09	$ 174.35	$ 99,139.74

Monthly Total for first year $ **7,923.61** $ **2,113.68**

The interest rate and twenty year payback were numbers chosen spontaneously and randomly for an example illustration to give you, the reader, the amortization schedule of payback of interest and principal as evidence to prove the sin of usury being perpetrated. Needless to say, we were very surprised and very amazed that the first monthly payment for the interest which would show this sin, was the mark of the beast, "666." In the writing of this book many confirmations encouraged and inspired its writing.

Note that nearly $8,000 of interest goes to the bank in the first twelve months! Only about $2,000.00 goes toward paying against your home! No wonder, God showed the first interest payment was '666', to speak to us. As Our Lady says:

March 25, 1990

>**"...God wants to save you and sends you messages through men, nature, and so many things which can only help you to understand that you must change the direction of your life..."**

First five months of year 12

Payment No.	Due Date	Payment	Interest	Principal	Balance
133	Jan, 2022	$ 836.44	$ 428.33	$ 408.11	$ 63,840.89
134	Feb, 2022	$ 836.44	$ 425.61	$ 410.83	$ 63,430.06
135	Mar, 2022	$ 836.44	$ 422.87	$ 413.57	$ 63,016.49
136	Apr, 2022	$ 836.44	$ 420.11	$ 416.33	$ 62,600.16
137	May, 2022	$ 836.44	$ 417.33	$ 419.11	$ 62,181.05

Monthly Total for year 12	$ 4,956.32	$ 5,080.96
End of 12th yr total to date	$ 79,615.40	$ 40,831.96

This is your loan and at the end of 12 years, you have paid double in interest than what you have paid against your house! It is enough to make one angry, like Jesus was angry in the temple. Yet, our pulpits are silent. Jesus' anger over the money changers in the temple didn't hurt anyone except those it should have. We need some of this Jesus anger from the pulpits, before people begin to get angry at the pulpit's silence. Pray and encourage the courageous priests who speak and are persecuted.

Incredibly, it takes 11½ years for the interest payback to drop below principal payback. Who devised and set these figures? To whose advantage? Study these figures carefully. And answer the following question of what banks do. If it looks like usury, smell likes usury, sounds like usury, is it or is it not usury?

By the end of 12 years, you have paid 80% of the bank's interest back and only 40% of your home's principal! 80%! to the bank, 40% against the home. 80/40 — is this not supreme usury? The defense would be, "Well when you compound the interest monthly, that is what the figures work out to be!" That's the point. Who decides it should be monthly or yearly compounded as if the loan end was each month or each year and you paid it off at the end of each of those periods. A **true** 8% loan, though still not moral, would be for the entire 20 years. That would be $33.33 interest per month. That would be a flat 8% of $100,000.00. But there's not enough big money to be made paying a one time interest for the whole $100,000.00, so the banks justify through "time value." A code word for usury. By compounding monthly, the banks achieve a new loan and its payoff of interest each month. It is, in reality, a singular loan per month. The 20 year (240 months) loan is actually 240 loans! If you make it honest, one may say, the bank may not make enough money. Why be concerned about that? It's the people who are being taken. It's precisely why Jefferson said:

> "And I sincerely believe…that banking establishments are more dangerous than standing armies."[70]

Yes, 33, the year Christ died; the three persons in the Holy Trinity. Our Lady for years says in Her messages, three times the word pray: pray, pray, pray. When you take 'time value', which justifies usury, out of the equation, the monthly interest payback amount is $33.33 per month. A number which arbitrarily came up!! $8,000.00 divided by 240 months (20 years)=$33.33 per month interest. How is that for confirmation? What are chances that 666 is the first interest payment of the monthly compounded loan and using the same exact amounts, borrowed at 8% interest, $33.33 is the amount when time value/usury (monthly compounding) is removed! This 33 sign should not be seen as affirmation that it is okay to borrow—it is still usury. The 33 should be seen as a sign of encouragement that we are headed toward the correct thinking away from usury.

Final 20th Year

First five months of year 20

Payment No.	Due Date	Payment	Interest	Principal	Balance
229	Jan, 2030	$ 836.44	$ 64.10	$ 772.34	$ 8,843.13
230	Feb, 2030	$ 836.44	$ 58.95	$ 777.49	$ 8,065.64
231	Mar, 2030	$ 836.44	$ 53.77	$ 782.67	$ 7,282.97
232	Apr, 2030	$ 836.44	$ 48.55	$ 787.89	$ 6,495.08
233	May, 2030	$ 836.44	$ 43.30	$ 793.14	$ 5,701.94

Monthly Total for 20th Year $ **421.73** $ **9,615.47**

End of 20th yr Total To Date $ **100,744.98** $ **100,000.00**

Before the January payment is made, as the first of the last 12 payments of the 20 year loan the balance still owed on your home is approximately ten thousand dollars. While what you owe the bank is approximately four hundred dollars. The bank, for several years previous to the 20th year has substantially taken "their" money, while you still owe substantially your balance of the "money" you borrowed! If you were to become ill, lose your source of income, and could not come up with $10,000 in this last year, you lose your home and the bank loses nothing. They still own your home as collateral. Is this evil usury? By participating in this, you become its collaborator. satan can strangle you with the rope you provided.

Are all bankers bad? No. They are people just like everyone else in a system that has standardized financing as respectable rather than morally abhorrent usury.

Now, as this chapter began, ask yourself if someone came up to you to loan you $100,000 two-hundred forty times, would you still say to him, "Do you think I'm a fool?" Would you still 'die laughing?' No, you would do neither, knowing that the mortgage you now have on your house, your car, etc., is indeed a monthly loan where you have been scammed, not just a little but severely scammed. An amount like the above $100,744.98 + $100,000 = $200,744.98. This loan is 100.7% interest.

It is a bold, blatant lie to say it is an 8% loan. In no stretch of the imagination can it be said this is an 8% loan. This lie was conceived in financial boardrooms. Our Lady wants you to know this. Go break down your own mortgage. Wake up to the sin of usury.

Look and study the figures on the previous pages. Once you learn what usury is, you would have to be, as Scripture speaks, 'a fool,' not to see this as point blank usury for your cars, house, everything you are borrowing for. If the Church can culturally accommodate that **which She doesn't approve of**, at the same time, contradicting ecclesiastical councils of Arles 314 A.D., Nicea 325 A.D., Carthage 348 A.D. and the first council of Aix 789 A.D., in which usury was denounced, then the Church can now accommodate Our Lady of Medjugorje's call to come back to the Christian life of living Biblical principles.

We all, as God's people, no longer see sin and that which is drowning us and the world. Our Lady said:

February 17, 1984

"...The world has been drawn into a great whirlpool. It does not know what it is doing. It does not realize in what sin it is sinking. It needs your prayers so that I can pull it out of this danger."

Wake up, O people of God. Think of the path we are on. Look and meditate on the three 6/24s. There is no way Our Lady appears **6/24**/81, and later asks us every Thursday to read **Matthew 6:24**, particularly, which thirdly, connects to an action on **6/24**/68, that broke the bonds for a world economy to exponentially expand, that has now enslaved man. These three revelations concerning the three 6:24s is revelation!* The Book of Revelation is about what will happen in the last times. The June 25, 1989, message of enslavement is what the Book of Revelation speaks of, that you will neither be able to buy nor sell without consenting to the mark of the beast. Our Lady's purpose behind these dates is to help us recognize the signs of the times. Our Lady came to forestall satan's time by waking us up to break his shackles of enslavement because this is Her time, and She actually alludes that She is here to crush the serpent's head, who is building this anti-christ system. Thereby, Our Lady is giving us the possibility of a reprieve, a short time of forestalling the time of the antichrist. Our Lady says:

December 25, 1999

"...Through your 'yes' for peace and your decision for God, a new possibility for peace is

---

* New revelation ceased with the death of the last apostle. The writer here expresses revelation in the discovery of a revelation that has always been there.

opened. Only in this way, little children, this century will be for you a time of peace and well-being..."

Read slowly and in prayer and seek the profoundness and greatness of the following message'**s**':

March 25, 1996

"Dear children! I invite you to decide again to love God above all else. In this time, when due to the spirit of consumerism, one forgets what it means to love and to cherish <u>true values</u>, I invite you again, little children, to put God in the first place in your life. Do not let satan attract you through material things but, little children, decide for God who is 'freedom' and love. Choose life and not death of the soul...that your life may be renewed today through conversion that shall lead you to eternal life..."

June 25, 1989

"Pray because you are in great temptation and danger because the world and material goods lead you into slavery. satan is active in this plan..."

May 2, 2009

"...My poor children, look around you and look at the signs of the times..."

Man completed a creation out of thin air on **6/24**, 1968, 'a **fiat money**.' Man in his arrogance contrasts God the Creator. Man cannot command and create as God can command and create. As the following shows, man acts out of darkness and falsehood. God acts out of light and truth.

Webster defines the word 'fiat':

>*Let it be done.*

The book of Genesis says in Chapter 1 that God said:

>*Let there be light.*

Webster defines fiat money:

>*Money, as paper currency, not convertible into coin of equivalent value.*

In the book of Genesis 1:18:

>*Divide the light from the darkness.*

Man speaks as God:

>*Let it be done.*

The lie is accomplished and sealed **6/24**. As God divided light from darkness, man mimics the truth with false truth by diverting silver backed currency to currency without worth. Paper without any value replaces true value, which was the dollar, backed by silver. This begins an unprecedented march toward the enslavement of man by his new master. It is an enslavement over the whole world, especially over the common man, inciting the love of money.

March 18, 1985

> **"...Right now many are greatly seeking money, not only in the parish, but in the whole world..."**

Our Lady teaches through these three 6/24 revelations:

Divide the light from the darkness.

Our Lady has come to show us, to teach us in order to help us see that which is from light and that which is from darkness, just as Claude Newman, the murderer, came from darkness to seeing the light, becoming a saint, through the grace of the Miraculous Medal. It is Our Lady who said in 1989 that satan has plans to make you a slave. She reiterates and tells us point blank that satan, the monkey of God, is 'active' in this plan to enslave you. This is in our generation, 1989! Yet, we buy the lie. People fall in line with the economic structure without questioning it at all. And people are actually praying the Prayers of the Faithful at Mass for the 'resurrection' or recovery of the economy! We need instead to be praying and preparing for a new way of life that is coming. Where is the light of wisdom? Blinded by greatly seeking money, Our Lady is showing all cultures who are riding in the car to <u>get out</u>, and now many are beginning to see what Our Lady has been saying all along.

February 25, 2000

"...Wake up from the sleep of unbelief and sin..."

Our unbelief of what is true has led us to sin and a declining culture. 1 Timothy 6:10:

"For the love of money is the root of all evils."

Scripture does not say roots of 'some evils,' rather 'all evils.' Money should not be what we pursue. A way of life, without the need of money, is what should be pursued.

People must meet their needs, not by seeking money, but by getting away from dependency upon it as much as possible through the efforts of their own labor, cou-

pled with community. No debt. Sustain yourself. Grow
your own food. Downsize. Live in a trailer while building your own home, if you must. Pay as you go. God
ordained this way of life for man, this way of producing
for oneself and one's family by his own labor, in the
very beginning when He said to Adam in the book of
Genesis that in toil he should bring forth and eat the
fruits of the earth. *"By the sweat of your brow shall
you eat"* (Genesis 3:19). There are hundreds of ways to
begin building your life according to the new time we
are coming into. Pray to understand what you can do to
change your life so as not to be dependent on the economic system. And don't think you have a lot of time
to make a decision. Our Lady has repeated, for almost
30 years, that you must change the direction of your life.
You are on the wrong path. You have taken a path of
misery, a path of ruin. You do not have time to procras-
tinate. Yesterday was the time to make a decision. In
other words, start now! It is a path to peace. It takes
years to build a new way of life. He who does not start
today, on this new way, will have a bitter, very bitter pill
to swallow if he delays a change of life based in Our
Lady's messages because of clinging to the hope for the
present economic disorder to revive. You are running
the clock out on your ability to make changes that will
not be possible in the future. Our Lady said:

November 2, 2006

> **"Dear children! My coming to you, my children, is God's love. God is sending me to warn you and to show you the right way. Do not shut your eyes before the truth, my children. <u>Your time is a short time.</u> Do not permit delusions to begin to rule over you. The way on which I desire to lead you is the way of peace and love. This is the way which leads to my Son, your God…"**

Did you read Our Lady's words? The greatness is that She is speaking clearly, warning you that you have a short time. Start the path to peace now! Do not think you cannot change things. We know many, many people who are following Our Lady, many who clearly understand that the present way of living is passing quickly away, and yet they still take no steps to change their way of living to be in accord with the fast approaching new time. So many let themselves become overwhelmed thinking there is too much that must be done or that it is too late, and this leads to a dangerous paralysis and resigned continuation of the same way of life. **No!** Don't be overwhelmed and slip into paralysis. Our Lady so often says, **"Dear children, _today!_"** She wants us to start now, even if we feel far behind. Take the first baby step, and then follow with more little steps. Just as with a little child, each baby step builds strength and confidence to take larger, more advanced steps. Begin with serious prayer. Start today! Begin praying eight mysteries* of the Rosary each day. What? Yes, eight, to give your heart clarity to give you the way out when there is no way out. Prayer can get you out of the most impossible situations. Our Lady said:

March 28, 1985

> **"...In prayer you shall perceive the greatest joy and the way out of every situation that has no exit..."**

Don't stop praying until Our Lady lights up the path you should take which will give you an exit, and then continue praying all the more. But still is it too much to ask to pray two full Rosaries* a day? Though it is true that in the beginning of the apparitions, Our Lady did not ask so much from the villagers of Medjugorje, we must remember that was 30 years ago. Over the years, progress has been made in Our Lady unveiling the future to us. We now have little time left. Though you can't immediately assimilate 30 years of messages and experiences with Our Lady on your own, you can make great advances in understanding Our Lady's call

---

* One complete Rosary, or four mysteries, is the Joyful, Luminous, Sorrowful, and Glorious Mysteries. Eight mysteries would be two complete Rosaries per day..

through the wisdom and understanding shared by those who have walked with Our Lady all these years. But you must pray and pray a lot. Even the visionaries complained to Our Lady when She asked for 4 hours of prayer a day. Our Lady said:

May 1984

Jelena tells Our Lady that if she tells the people to pray four hours a day they will back out.

"Don't you understand, that it is only one-sixth of the day?"

Our Lady repeatedly says to pray unceasingly. St. Paul says to pray without ceasing. You must create a daily prayer life. If you haven't begun one already, start today. If you already pray daily, you must increase your prayers in order to be illuminated as to the decisions you are to make. If you don't have time in your day, you must make time, even if that means waking up one hour earlier daily, plus eliminating other things from your schedule.

Does this read seem a long way away from where this writing began about the Miraculous Medal and the special Miraculous Medal Medjugorje message? No, you actually have made a full circle and are back at the beginning. Then what does all this mean? It means we've got a short window of time to spread Our Lady's Miraculous Medal Medjugorje message of November 27, 1989, for your benefit and well-being, and other's spiritual and physical well-being! Read again this message. But read it with all that you've been enlightened by through this writing, and seek to comprehend the profoundness and the greatness of putting this message into life — into your life and into others' lives. This includes the lives of those you do not know, and the lives of generations yet to be born who will know you not, nor will you know of, but having passed through this life you will have a direct effect upon their conversions.

November 27, 1989

> **"These days, I want you to pray in a special way for the salvation of souls. Today is the feast day of the Miraculous Medal, and I want that you pray, in a special way, for the salvation of those people who are carrying this Miraculous Medal. I want you to spread the devotion and the carrying of this medal, so that more souls may be saved, and that you pray in a special way."**

In the next chapters you will learn of a remarkable way you can affect, with the above message, people in the present and those whose lives will come after you when you are long gone from the earth. We have an opportunity to implement this message in an incredible way, a way that benefits your spiritual and physical well being! Our Lady said January 25, 2009:

> **"...for all worldly things** (are) **to be a help for you to draw you closer to God the Creator..."**

July 25, 1988

> **"...Everything you do and everything you possess give over to God so that He can take control in your life as King of all that you possess..."**

CHAPTER FIFTEEN

It Cannot.
It Never Has.
It Never Will.

W hen the backing of silver was stripped from the dollar on 6/24/68, the stage was being set for the woes that have befallen us now. It is not to say this action was the beginning or the start of a fall, for modern man, on a wide scale, already had love of money in his heart before 6/24/68 and so God permitted such, giving man up to himself and his desires. Now we have an integrated slave-holding economy where almost all are in shackles, represented by an out of control car headed down the mountain with no brakes.

As stated earlier, in the history of the entire world, no paper currency, which was not backed by gold or silver, lasted more than 50 years. 6/24/68 was 42 years ago. Again, this is being written in April/May 2010. Why will the fiat system not last? Michael Maroney of Monex Metals, made the statement below in 2005. Since that time, figures have gigantically, exponentially increased with the stimulus funds for bailouts, not just in the United States, but other nations as well. Maroney states:

> *"Over the course of history, all great societies have eventually created unsustainable amounts of debt and because of that governments are forced to print money. And if you look at the circumstances that currently exist in the United States, you've heard about the stock bubble, you've heard about the housing bubble, but nobody's really talking about the debt bubble that exists. Our government has a published debt of $8.5 trillion, but if you add in additional liabilities such as social security, medicare, pension guarantee programs, it's estimated to be upwards of $45 trillion. Then if you add in Federal, State, municipalities, county, consumer, corporate, our debt right now is close to being at the $50 trillion level. There is absolutely no way for this country to exist unless we continue to print money.*

> *"It is imperative to understand that paper currencies depreciate. I think it's easily said this way — that paper money becomes worth less and worth less and then it becomes worthless. Now based on that premise if we go back to what happened in the 1980's, early 1980 we had silver*

that went roughly from the $2 level in the early 70's up to $50 an ounce for a 25 fold increase. Right now what we have is a money supply increase from 1980 to right now of about 7 times as much. Well, silver reached $50 an ounce when there was 1.5 billion ounces more available in the market than there is now. (Now there is only approximately 771 million ounces of bullion, as of April/May 2010. [71])

"There's only 800 billion dollars in America in cash (again all figures stated in 2005 and have grown exponentially) *and out of that we somehow get an $11 trillion economy. We have currently a personal debt of the United States people of about $30 trillion. There is a derivative hedge book out there of $450 trillion. We have a current account deficit of $800 billion a year. We've got a budget deficit of a loan of $600 billion and that's not even most of it. The majority of Federal spending comes in supplemental requests and off-budget things. It comes out to over a trillion dollars per year in an $11 trillion economy. How can you do that? That's the part that's so staggering to me that people actually believe that*

this will work out. **It cannot. It never has and it never will.**

"The government is going to have to take on more and more debt to keep this game going. So I think deficits that appear to be high now are going materially higher, which again is good for precious metals."[72]

And so a very unique spiritual opportunity 'and' physical opportunity exists in this particular time, possibly for a short duration of time.

If you have any money in savings, stocks, in any holdings, you can use your money for the salvation of souls, for the spiritual well-being of others as well as, at the same time, for your own spiritual and physical well-being without it costing you.

Experts, as well as almost everyone else, are predicting hyperinflation, then radical deflation. Inflation actually has already begun due to the incredible amount of fiat money being printed. As the dollar becomes worth less and less, you will have a harder time keeping up, because the dollars you saved or invested or what you bring home week to week from your take home pay will be losing value. Experts say silver wins both ways as it tends to keep up with inflation, but in periods of deflation will always have worth. So you do not lose as you would with the dollar. In other words, in regards to inflation, if you have $36.00 and you take half, putting $18.00 in the bank, and with the other $18.00 obtain one ounce of silver, what will happen? Suppose next year inflation turned your bank deposit of $18.00 cash dollars into $10.00 in value. What would happen with the one troy ounce of silver? The prevailing thought is, historically, it would stay up with inflation and may even exceed the inflation rate. Accordingly, then silver should lose no value and if there is a price correction, you may gain much, much more against inflation. Silver will always have value. If or when silver's price per ounce corrects in relation to gold to its historical price ratio of approximately 15 times, its value could rise to be $80.00 per ounce, or even more depending upon actual supplies. Factoring in the dynamics of the fiat paper money becoming worthless through hyperinflation and shortages, silver could go much higher according to its demand and competition from industry, making the market rise. If silver reserves and mining production cannot keep up with the demand, this also will affect the value of silver, making it go still higher. Remember, as already shown in this writing on page 124, history shows no fiat system ever lasted

more than 50 years. Where are we in the 50 year limit
of our current paper currency? We are in the final
eight years, maximum, if the fiat money will even last
that long, as of May 12, 2010. That is the maximum,
history has told us, paper money, fiat money, can last.
History does not lie. Many different sources and
pieces of information indicate that silver is, at this
writing, being purposefully manipulated to suppress
it from rising to its historical value, keeping the price
down 65 times per ounce less than the cost of gold.[73]
Don't just take these written words about these facts.
Research it yourself. You will find everything written
in these pages to be factual. After the book was written, extensive research on each fact for this book was
performed with a team of five to validate and authen-
ticate to make sure the facts were facts.* Yet, as you
research, you will find silver is also being depleted
through countless irretrievable uses in thousands of
products like cell phones, washing machines, etc., all
of which affects supply and demand, raising silver's
price.

---

* The author did not accept the 'experts' or the estimates for sources. For this writing, he assembled a research team to verify sources. He researched the source
of the information of why the presented facts were facts. He does not claim the
writings to be without the possibility of some margin of error. However, the information is as verifiable as can be done in answering the what, who, and why of
the sources, tracing the facts back to the original sources.

According to the World Silver Survey 2009, aside from industry usage, coins, jewelry, and individual private stocks, at present there are only approximately 771 million ounces of above ground silver bullion that can be counted of the 47.9 billion ounces that have been brought to the surface from mining throughout man's history. Aside from industry usage, coins, jewelry, and private or governmental stocks, there are approximately 955 million ounces of above ground gold bullion that can be counted available to potential purchasers.[74] Therefore, the above ground known reserve of silver is actually more rare than the known reserve of above ground gold bullion because there are fewer ounces of silver bullion than gold bullion above ground!

The Silver Eagle coin broke all its prior sales records at the U.S. Mint in the first quarter of 2010. The mint sold 9,023,500 of the coins in the first quarter, which is more than any other quarter period since the Silver Eagle was introduced.[75] If such sales were to continue, the minting of these coins alone in 2010 would require approximately 90% of the entire annual U.S. mine production of silver![76] What will industry do since 45% of silver production is consumed for their products? The stress on U.S. supply would require even greater silver purchases from foreign holders, thereby raising prices. As stated, the United States Geological 2009 Survey states that all below ground silver, at current mine production rates, will be mined in an estimated 18.5 years. That is all the silver left in the ground.

Caritas began speaking of silver on their Radio Wave program, *Mejanomics*, hosted on their website, Medjugorje.com, in the fall of 2008. The importance of buying silver was discussed. Since then, there has been an ongoing discussion about it in talks on Medjugorje. com, as well as in writings and in retreats. According to the Silver Institute, world coin and medal demand for silver has averaged 43 million ounces per year over the last ten years.[77]

Caritas is responsible for over 900,000 ounces being purchased last year through its outreach and Biblical guidance. This is over 2% of world demand for coins and medals! And this figure is only what we can verify. Others who listen in on *Mejanomics* radio programs or who have heard through other outreaches of Caritas, such as through the Caritas Newsletter, talks and retreats, who buy silver without our knowledge, we have no way of knowing the amount of ounces they've traded their dollars in for. It appears those who are praying, reflecting on their future, who recognize the signs of the times, immediately understand what has been voiced on *Mejanomics* and more so on what will be released through these pages as to why they are transferring what they have into silver.

CHAPTER SIXTEEN

The Unique Opportunity

A return to truth, a return to Our Lady's call to cherish true values, certainly means a return to morality, Christian ethics, and incorporating Christian principles into daily life, but it also means what 6/24, 6:24, 6/24 reveals to us. You are to use:

January 25, 2009

> **"…'all' worldly things to be a help for you to draw you closer to God the Creator…"**

You can take your money, no matter how meager, and put it into silver as a promising way to keep its value and, at the same time, promote Our Lady's November 27, 1989, Miraculous Medal message, putting it into life.

After our eyes were opened about Our Lady's Miraculous Medal Medjugorje message of November 27, 1989, we immediately had the desire to evangelize the Miraculous Medal and message. Through prayer, a new method of evangelization evolved, just as the statement in the The Poem of the Man-God revealed that "new methods of evangelization" would be incorporated that the world has never seen before, for the final Great Evangelization the world will ever see.

A new design for the Miraculous Medal that ties to Medjugorje and Our Lady's apparitions has been minted on a silver round. The silver round ties images of Medjugorje and sites of Our Lady's apparitions with information to learn more about Medjugorje on both the front and the back, together with the Miraculous Medal minted upon it. Many do not know what to put their funds or investments in to keep them safe. We went to work and designed a one troy ounce round of .999 refined silver* that everyone could place their money into. What is indicated by the circumstances we find ourselves in is that your money sitting in the bank is decreasing in value through inflation, and as part of the paper fiat system, this money will eventually completely crash, becoming worthless. When that happens, silver will continue to be used as a means of exchange. You can have the Miraculous Medal Medjugorje Round in your possession for your own physical welfare as well as to help evangelize those who will have these rounds fall into their possession. Our Lady's messages relay

---

* The highest amount of pure silver **.999 pure silver; the other .001 is copper, which must be added to give it strength.**

to use all temporal goods to serve and help populate Heaven. The one ounce silver piece minted will eventually trickle out and be 'carried' even by non-believers. When Claude Newman grabbed hold of the Miraculous Medal, a "new possibility for peace opened" to him, even though he was totally without knowledge of Jesus, much less the Virgin Mary. With the Miraculous Medal in his possession, he was led to conversion and then, he, in turn, converted the reprobate who hated him and who hated God. Some of those who in the future read this writing will also be counted among the converted because of the Miraculous Medal conversion of Claude Newman. Our Lady said:

November 27, 1989

"...I want that you pray, in a special way, for the salvation of those people who are carrying this Miraculous Medal..."

You can use your **'worldly things'** as Our Lady has asked, not only to help you draw closer to God, but others as well!

All this, with God's grace, will incorporate Our Lady's message of November 27, 1989 into life. The "spiritual and physical benefits" as a result of the one ounce

Spiritual Benefits {

1. Carrying of the Miraculous Medal. Bringing conversion.

2. Spreading the devotion, as Our Lady asks, for generations to come. Our Lady will be more known and loved.

3. Praying for the salvation of those souls, unbelievers, who carry the Miraculous Medal Medjugorje Round, which will initiate grace for conversions.

Physical Well-being {

1. Preserving the true value of what money you have saved or invested into silver because it has intrinsic value.

2. Many precious metal experts believe it will protect from inflation, and will still maintain value in deflation.

3. Benefitting from any correction as demand increases. Even if the price per ounce falls, it will never be valueless because in the event of an economic correction or collapse, silver will always be used as a means of preservation of assets, savings and/or an exchange of goods and services as it has been throughout history.

Miraculous Medal Medjugorje Round Silver piece includes:

There exists an incredible, unique opportunity in this time. Whether you put $18.00 or over $1,000,000.00 into the silver Miraculous Medal Medjugorje Rounds, when you cash it out, it will never be cast away because it has true value and even a non-believer or murderer like Claude Newman, who comes into its possession, will keep it and **"carry it"** because of its intrinsic value. The rest is in Our Lady's hands.

Our Lady said on November 27, 1989:

> **"...I want you to spread the devotion and the carrying of this medal, so that more souls may be saved..."**

Using a new method for evangelization, can your assets not work to bring souls to conversion for generations to come? The one ounce silver piece was officially released **'6/24,'** June 24, 2010. And yes, it worked out to that date. We tried to release it much earlier, but it was not possible. It ended up as the week of **6/24**, so we picked that day of the week! 'Confirmation of cooperation' with Our Lady. For the past two months, since it was first minted, those who previewed it, with Our Lady's message, immediately wanted it and begged that we would pre-release some. We wanted to wait until everything was laid out and the explanation of the purpose of striking a Miraculous Medal tied to the image of Our Lady of Medjugorje and Her apparitions could be clearly explained with its dual purpose of providing for the spiritual and physical well-being of those who hold them. With just a few of these rounds being pre-released, we have had a hard time waiting to officially release the struck one ounce Miraculous Medal Medjugorje Rounds because as the medal is shared, others are coming forward inquiring about them. Some have wanted, for some time, to get out of the stock market and have begun moving their stocks into the rounds, others their savings and/or other investments into the Miraculous Medal Medjugorje Round. All this together has already totaled over one million dollars in these special silver rounds. Others, as of this writing, have been waiting for the release and are planning to put from $100.00 to seven figures into the one ounce rounds. They all like the idea and concept that these silver rounds will eventually work their way into many hands in the next years and decades, working for many Claude Newman conversions for the worst non-believers. Others want to give them away, as was the tradition in many families only just a few decades ago, who gave the American Eagle Silver dollar to children receiving their First Holy Communion. Others in planning their wills, are giving these silver rounds as an inheritance to their children instead of cash. In addition, they are being given as true family heirlooms. Some are exchanging cash for the rounds because of what they have learned about silver through their own investigation, and desire a round dedicated to Our Lady over any other silver round they could obtain. Also, a whole support base through the mission of Caritas of Birmingham, as with Caritas' Billboard program, is ready to spiritually feed information about Medjugorje to those prompted by carrying the Miraculous Medal Medjugorje silver rounds. The work of the Community of Caritas, whose lives are full-time missionaries of Our Lady of Medjugorje's messages, both in witness and in work, will run this support base. This will be extensively supported by Caritas' web site, printing operation, and phone operation, the missionaries of the Community of Caritas, the Caritas Mission House in Medjugorje, and various other operations of Caritas.

Through the silver rounds' dual purpose, spiritual and physical, and by using a 'worldly thing,' the true value of this new evangelization project will produce tremendous fruit. Based in Our Lady's message, with God's grace, Our Lady's watchful glance, and your prayers in a special way for the salvation of souls who end up carrying the round — a host of people living mediocre Christianity will have the possibility of conversion. The serious non-believer or those ignorant of God, or in other words, the Claude Newmans of our

The Caritas Billboard program is a nationwide program now going to other countries, promoting Our Lady's Medjugorje apparitions. Caritas has strong contacts with some corporations who have collaborated with them to put up billboards about Our Lady and Her apparitions. Every 100 billboards placed up averages 3.5 million glances per day by those who pass by them. With over 1,000 billboards placed across America, by God's grace, Caritas has introduced Our Lady to millions of people. It does not end there. Caritas' network of printing, web site, specialized phone system, with 60 extensions all of which supports and feeds the souls who make inquiries from seeing the billboards, with free materials and information. As with the Billboard program, the silver round is another such spiritual "fishnet" to capture people for Our Lady through decades to come by doing the same, giving them free material, incited from the Miraculous Medal Medjugorje Round silver piece for the last Great Evangelization..

day, can all have the chance for salvation. Our Lady can use this tool for our time in bringing about a huge harvest of conversion. A new way (method) of evangelization in keeping with the time, without substantially changing the Gospel, as Maria Valtorta wrote in the The Notebooks, part of The Poem of the Man-God, and mentioned on page 48 of this book, which by rereading, your heart will be incited and excited of what a unique opportunity we have before us.

Our Lady's November 27, 1989, message to spread the Miraculous Medal is an incredible rejuvenation, reinvigoration of a past grace to be used today. While this writing was in progress, Our Lady made known another astonishing revelation about the whole dual purpose of evangelization and using one's means, wealth, or 'worldly things' to draw themselves and others close to God. It follows:

In the 150th anniversary of Our Lady giving the Miraculous Medal to St. Catherine, Pope John Paul II went, on May 31, 1980, to Rue du Bac's* Miraculous Medal Chapel, in Paris, France. There John Paul II inaugurated the:

"resumption of the cult" of the Miraculous Medal.[78]

---

* Rue du Bac is the name of the street where St. Catherine's chapel is located, where she lived, and where she received the apparition of the Miraculous Medal.

Webster defines cult: *Formal religious veneration:*
                            worship. A system of reli-
                            gious beliefs and rituals.

This act of John Paul II, at the beginning of the decade, cannot in any way be separated from Our Lady's strong steps at the end of the same decade on November 27, 1989, giving Marija a message, during the apparition for the ***"resumption of the cult"*** of the Miraculous Medal. A term used in the Church to resume the devotion or cult previously established. Rene Laurentin, a French Theologian, wrote of John Paul II's visit as the **"resumption of the cult."**

Scripture states in regards to the Church and the Chair of Peter in regards to Pope John Paul II's actions:

Matthew 16:19

> ***"Whatever you bind on earth shall be***
> ***bound in Heaven, and whatever you loose***
> ***on earth shall be loosed in Heaven."***

The act of inauguration by John Paul II on May 31, 1980, binds on earth the *"resumption of the cult"* of the Miraculous Medal. And the act of inauguration by Our Lady on November 27, 1989 message binds in Heaven, because of what was bound on earth, the *"resumption of the cult"* of the Miraculous Medal. These two inaugurations, tying the medal to Medjugorje, brings to life the Scripture, *"whatever you bind on earth shall be bound in Heaven."* But the real exciting revelation of this event is the definition of '**resumption**,' the 'resumption' of the cult, and what it uncovers.

Webster defines **resumption**: *An act of resuming, a return to payment in* **specie**.[79]

The astonishing revelation:

Webster defines **specie**:   *Money in coin*.[80]

The inauguration preformed by John Paul II in 1980 and Our Lady in 1989 was an act of resuming a return in specie, defined as a return to payment in money in coin. It cannot be clearer!

The above is an amazing revelation, in regard to striking these one ounce rounds.

6/24/81:   Apparitions begin. The call to love what is truth.

Matthew **6/24**:   The Scripture passage concerning God or money is to be read every Thursday: to protect us from the lie.

6/24/68:   Money no longer backed by coin (silver
              coins at that time).

The lie completed.

A resumption of the cult of the Miraculous Medal
by Pope John Paul II, May 31, 1980, and resumption of
the cult by Our Lady, November 27, 1989, back to true
value could only be a happening of God. Silver, having
miraculous qualities, is by the touch of its Creator. The
resumption of its ordained use, especially being used
for a holy purpose and with good will cannot but draw
souls closer to God and salvation. It gives protection,
both for your spiritual and physical well-being, and others besides. Seek first the Kingdom of God and all these
things will be given to you besides! Seeking the Kingdom of God brings the Kingdom of God. When the
Kingdom of God comes, a new possibility of peace and
well-being will reign. Our Lady said:

December 25, 1999

> **"...Through your 'yes' for peace and your de-
> cision for God, a new possibility for peace is
> opened. Only in this way, little children, this
> century will be for you a time of peace and well-
> being..."**

The date of the above message is December 25, 1999. In it, Our Lady references the turn of the millennium, and its first century. Whether She means exactly the first 100 years of the millennium or beginning sometime within the time of the twenty-first century, for sure She meant it will be for you a time of peace and well-being.

Your yes is required. Your comprehending what is true will make you want to say yes. It is then that one can begin to understand true value, spiritually and physically.

Fr. René Laurentin wrote of a particularly profound conversion that was the result of the Miraculous Medal. *"By the beginning of 1842, Catherine had heard a piece of news which was spreading like wildfire: all the presses were printing and talking about it. A young Jewish banker from Alsace, France, recently engaged to be married, had gone to Rome. Alphonse Ratisbonne was rather critical of Catholicism, but a French friend, Théodore de Bussières, challenged him to accept the medal and he was converted suddenly in the church of St. Andrea delle Fratte. The Virgin appeared to him, just as on the medal. "She said nothing to me," he said, "but I understood everything." This happened on January 20, and the new convert had already been received by Pope Gregory XV by the end of the month."*[81] Ratisbonne, the Jewish convert, then became a priest. The left picture

shows the actual Miraculous Medal that Ratisbonne was wearing at the time of his vision of the Blessed Virgin Mary and his conversion of faith. The Miraculous Medal is in safe-keeping in the religious congregation of Our Lady of Zion, located in the City of Evry in France. Alphonse Ratisbonne founded the order of Our Lady of Zion after becoming a priest. He continued to wear the Miraculous Medal of his conversion, but before his death, gave it over to the mother superior of the order, Mother M. Eléonore. She wore it for the rest of her life, and as she did not specify any person to receive it after her, the congregation framed the medal, as you see here pictured. *Following is the translation from the French Text:*

"We certify, after receiving it from Mother M. Eléonore, that this Miraculous Medal was worn by Father Marie on January 20, 1842. It was left by him to Mother Eléonore who wore it until the day of her death on December 28, 1930."[82]

When he became a priest Alphonse Ratisbonne became Fr. Marie.

Shown here is the interior of the church St. Andrea delle Fratte, where Alphonse Ratisbonne experienced his dramatic conversion. The bust shown on the left hand side is of Ratisbonne, placed on the exact spot where Our Lady appeared to him as depicted in the painting to the right.

Shown right is Medjugorje visionary, Marija Lunetti, giving away Miraculous Medals to pilgrims just after Our Lady blessed them during an apparition in the Field in Alabama. Thousands had gathered for five days of prayer to reconcile themselves, their families, and their nation back to God. Marija personally handed out over twelve thousand Miraculous Medals to thousands of individuals who were overwhelmed with joy to receive them from Marija just after Our Lady blessed them.

189

CHAPTER SEVENTEEN

Scruples

Before even beginning this writing, we knew there would be those who would be scandalized that an image of Our Lady was being placed upon a silver round. Some, because of their scruples, may have rejected this entire writing because they falsely believe it to be in bad taste to have Our Lady on anything that has to do with things of value. And yet, Our Lady gave a private message through Medjugorje visionary Marija, directly for and a command to the Caritas Community on May 31, 1995:

"...Get as many hearts as you can close to my heart and lead them to God, to a way of salvation..."

What hearts? Where should we look for them? By what means should we use to lead them to "a way of salvation?" Leaving pamphlets and brochures at the back of a church gives one an opportunity to learn of Medjugorje, but that's for those who go to church. What

of those who do not go to church? What of those who
are so engrossed in making money that they have little
time for anything else, whose lives end up in divorce and
broken families, illicit lifestyles, living without limits…
how are these souls to be reached? How do we enter
into the world of finance and wealth, or even into the
lives of gang members, the middle class, even the poor
who are 'greatly seeking money,' of which these souls, as
Mother Teresa once stated, live in greater poverty than
those who are dying in the streets of Calcutta.

Be it in the highest skyscraper of the rich and
wealthy, to the common man making an honest living, to
the gang member on the street, the Miraculous Medal
Medjugorje Round has a great potential, with the blessing of God, to enter into a world where 'mammon' is
the chosen god. But when that god fails to 'resurrect,'
who shall save these souls from despair? Can you not
imagine the impact of believers seeing the image of the
Virgin Mary with the Cross of Her Son upon a silver
medallion? Believers can, in turn, spread the Miraculous Medal Medjugorje Round in the world of high
stakes and high pressure, money, power, competition,
corruption, theft, slander, indictments, immoral living,
etc. Few would take a 'trinket,' as Claude Newman
thought of the Miraculous Medal which he put around

his neck. But no one would refuse to carry a one ounce silver round, even if used temporarily because it has intrinsic value in and of itself. These same rounds that will help you, in some degree, to secure your new way of life and its future, and then trickling down and out, will eventually be brought into the mainstream of usage, and then Our Lady will have an opportunity to lead a heart towards Her, through the prayers and sacrifices of Her children, of which Claude Newman was both a recipient of the grace attached to the Miraculous Medal and a conduit of grace for not only the reprobate's conversion, but several other conversions as well.

For those who still may have scruples, consider the fact that when St. Catherine's medal was cast, and millions of these medals were made, that it cost money. Money was spent in producing the medals, and many people, as well, spent money to acquire them. And yet these medals that were produced with money and purchased with money produced so many miracles, thousands and thousands of them, that the medal became known as the Miraculous Medal. Go to any religious pilgrimage site around the world and you will find religious articles for sale, along with Miraculous Medals. The cynic will immediately complain that people are taking advantage of a religious event to make money, but the reality is that often times when someone experiences conversion during a religious pilgrimage, they may purchase rosaries or medals, have them blessed and then give them away as gifts to those they hope will also experience conversion. But the amazing thing is that God will use the gift that was bought with money to open someone's heart to grace. It's not the money, but rather, what is in the heart that counts. A heart filled with good will and a desire to see someone's conversion who needs it, will see their desires fulfilled through grace, by using an opportunity Our Lady gives to reach a soul.

This is the beauty of Claude Newman's story. The medal that was worn by the first prisoner, who discarded it, and then was taken possession of by Claude cost money to someone—both the producer and the purchaser. Yet, Our Lady used it to save not just the soul of Claude Newman and James Hughes, but it impacted Fr. O'Leary, the Sheriff and the District Attorney, and the other prisoners as well. And the conversion continued to trickle out as in the same morning that James Hughes was executed, there was the woman prisoner executed beforehand, the first woman ever to be executed in the state of Mississippi, also for murder. And remember before the moment of her death, she caught the eye of the priest in attendance, and she smiled. She had converted to Catholicism in the past few months, and had made her peace with God. It was Claude Newman that moved the two religious sisters to become interested in coming down to the jail to speak with the women prisoners and teach them the faith. How many others were there that were saved in this time? What have we learned about Our Lady through these events? That She would go into the pit of hell itself, if She could save a soul. Imagine Her descending into the cells of these criminals of society, who had murdered and committed other unmentionable crimes against God, men, and themselves—and Our Lady comes to them with mercy, love, compassion and the offer of salvation. And how many who will read of Claude's story will be brought to conversion? All these 'miracles' through one, only one, just one Miraculous Medal. What is waiting for the Miraculous Medal Medjugorje Round?

Because of your scruples, don't limit God in what circumstances He will enter to save a soul. It has been our experience over nearly a quarter of a century since being involved with Medjugorje that Our Lady wants to cooperate with Her children to save souls, just as She said on August 4, 1988:

"...I want your cooperation. I want to work with you. Your cooperation is necessary to me. I cannot do anything without you."

New bold moves for evangelization fit the above '**cooperation**' message, but yet how do we know for sure? Because Our Lady also told us on August 26, 1996, as with the May 31, 1995 message quoted at the beginning of this chapter, a message directly to the Community of Caritas, a private message through the visionary, Vicka. We presented a novena that was being prayed by the Community of Caritas for the visionaries, villagers, and village of Medjugorje that Vicka presented on August 26, 1996, asking Our Lady if She would accept it. Our Lady said:

"Whatever you are doing with the heart, it is all precious to Me."

Our personal experiences with Our Lady showed us, with this message, it is the heart that matters in what makes grace rain down and brings forth fruit for what is done for Her because, **"...it is <u>all</u> precious..."** A project of conversion is our hearts' longing. No other confirmation or confirmation from anyone is needed to cooperate with Our Lady's last great evangelization.

Every spiritual project of the heart that we have for-
mulated here, inspired by Our Lady, through the Holy
Spirit, over the years to bring conversion to souls has
been blessed with abundant fruit, far surpassing all our
expectations. And with every idea, there were always
the naysayers, always based in jealousy, giving reasons
why the idea wouldn't work, shouldn't work, or why
God wouldn't allow it, nor bless it. They often used what
means they had at their disposal to denounce publicly
the projects, try to harm or try to destroy the project
by shrouding our promotion with suspicion in order to
discourage people from praying, monetarily supporting
or working with such new and unique evangelization
efforts. This project won't be any different. But our
history has shown over and over again God's blessing
upon each project, and the mission itself. Caritas has a
long history of our cooperation with Our Lady, and Her
cooperating with our efforts to **"get hearts close to Her
Heart."** We believe the Miraculous Medal Medjugorje
Silver Round will far surpass all our hopes in leading
souls to conversion. It is with this hope and intention
of heart that we launch this project. If Our Lady could
use one Miraculous Medal to wrench from satan's grasp
those awaiting their execution on death row, then what
will She do for those on the other side of the spectrum,
who are believers, yet equally in the grasp of satan be-

cause of their choice to serve the mammon of the present economic disorder, instead of God? And also unbelievers besides!

Another point which must be addressed to those who object, saying, "one cannot sell blessed objects." We are not advocating selling anything as being blessed. But what if it is blessed, does that mean one cannot trade it for dollars? Houses are blessed often, yet sold, lands also. What about vehicles that have been blessed, or the blessing of the fleets, and other boats? One cannot sell something as the reason of its blessing. Many things are sold that have been blessed. Yet still, we do not advocate blessing the rounds and selling them because they are blessed, as this is against Church law.

With St. Catherine's medal, the Bishop, after many delays finally ordered the medal to be cast, saying that they would watch to see what would happen. In the end, that is all that we can do with the Miraculous Medal Medjugorje Round. We will promote it and spread it, but the rest is in Our Lady's hands as to how She will use it to bring about conversion of souls. But remember the saints who were given visions of hell, one of which said she would die 1,000 torturous deaths to save one soul from hell so horrible it is. This project will be a total success, if only one soul is saved from hell.

(Chapter 18 continues on page 205).

The mission of Caritas of Birmingham is operated by the Community of Caritas. It is their life. Literally countless mailings, millions of books, booklets, and other Medjugorje support material of Our Lady's messages have been mailed out, much of it free, supported by their Field Angel program. These mailings are processed through equipment from presses, folders, cutters, forklift, package sorting and many other machines. Each piece of equipment is consecrated and marked with a Miraculous Medal glued on it. Even their lands have Miraculous Medals blessed by Our Lady buried across them. Above is mail being processed to go to as many as 120 countries. Below, the mail with hands imposed upon it is being prayed over to receive Our Lady's blessing by proxy for those who are spiritually hungry and for the material to heal those who are spiritually sick. Our Lady says to impose hands on the sick. Spiritual disease and mentalities are the number one disease that needs healing today.

July 25, 1982

"…It is good to impose one's hands on the sick and to pray…"

This is Caritas' work and its mission which operates out of *the Tabernacle of Our Lady's messages.*

The Tabernacle of Our Lady's Messages in Alabama is the motherhouse of the Medjugorje mission of Caritas of Birmingham, operated by the Community of Caritas. From the foundation to the stone work, there are countless Miraculous Medals and other blessed objects cemented in its floors and walls. Caritas is the largest Medjugorje center in the world and at present, 2010, is undergoing an extensive expansion, doubling the size of the print shop, shipping and many other areas to increase further their capability to "missionary" Our Lady's work and prayer life throughout the world, one heart at a time. The 55,000 square foot facility's purpose is to serve and propagate Our Lady Queen of Peace of Medjugorje's messages around the world, and help others, through free materials, to do the same.

The new project of the Miraculous Medal Medjugorje Round is just one of many ways the mission of Caritas spreads and helps others to implement Our Lady's messages and transform them into life. Our Lady said;

December 25, 1989:

"…read everyday the messages I gave you and transform them into life…"

The Tabernacle of Our Lady's Messages is a place of life.

About the Pictures

Every piece of equipment and building Caritas has is marked with the Miraculous Medal. The medals glued on (right) signifies their consecration to Our Lady to advance the mission of Caritas for the conversion of the world. The prayers are prayed while the Community imposes hands. This consecration is acknowledgement of God's ownership and Caritas' stewardship of each gift so that in humility the proper order is professed of who is the Giver and Creator and who is the receiver and gifted user. The typical prayer prayed by the founder of Caritas while the Miraculous Medal is being permanently attached follows:

God, this machine, two hundred years ago, was nothing but minerals in the earth. It was scattered across whatever origins it is from. Your laws of physics brought it together to a new form, not through what man invented, but what he discovered You had invented and created through physics. This equipment came together, these parts, this metal, this plastic, this steel, all from the earth which is Your domain, a domain which You own. Through Your genius, that You placed in the earth eons ago, in the beginning of creation, these minerals and elements have come together to form this machine. How prideful it is for us to ever think this came from us, or that this is some kind of new invention of man. This is the touch of You as our God, it is of Your creation, it is of You! We, therefore, worship You for this thing that has Your touch and Your beauty of creation crafted into it. We consecrate it to You, that what comes from this equipment will lead to conversions, graces, and holiness to change the direction of the world in bringing about a simple way of life. We thereby put this medal on what you have made and granted in order to consecrate it and give it back to You through Our Lady. With this consecration, we formerly give You titleship of it, as a reminder to us that it has no origins from man as we are from dust and unto dust we shall return. Therefore this machine of the dust and minerals laid in the earth, now formed, cannot be claimed by genius of man, but rather, in our hearts, we always comprehend it is Yours for Our Lady's use for the salvation of the world. Amen.

From small tools to the largest presses in Caritas' print shop throughout the mission, all is given to Our Lady for Her purposes, Her plans, and Her wishes. Everything the Community possesses belongs to Our Lady to advance Her plans for the salvation of the world, based in Our Lady's message of July 25, 1988:

"...Everything you do and everything you possess give over to God so that He can take control in your life as King of all that you possess..."

The new four story expansion of the Tabernacle of Our Lady's Messages is prayed over and a Miraculous Medal, blessed by Our Lady, is glued to one of its structural beams by Community members. The walls have blessed medals and rosaries in the concrete. Those blessed objects were sent by supporters of Our Lady's mission to Caritas from all over to become part of the new expansion of Our Lady's Tabernacle. Below picture was taken July, 2010. This extension will greatly expand Caritas' capability for spiritual projects such as the Miraculous Medal Medjugorje Round, in promotion of Our Lady's messages.

Above: Our Lady's statue overlooks one of the presses in Caritas' print shop, where every piece of equipment has a Miraculous Medal glued upon it. Below: The Community of Caritas surrounds a large piece of equipment to consecrate it to Our Lady while a Miraculous Medal is glued to the inside of its instrument panel. Our Lady's whole plan is to lead the world back to Her Son. In the near future, we will see a new grace cover the entire world. Our Lady is building a following of all God's children, though many are unaware that She is the one drawing them together. One day She will be made known and at just the right moment, She will step aside, and there will be Jesus standing with open arms. Just as Jesus was born at the right moment in Bethlehem, He will be "born again" in hearts, instantly, in an unprecedented illumination that will be given not only to Christians who will be reconverted to the real life of Jesus and the following of the Commandments in a fuller way, but also to non-believers, Muslims, Hindus, etc., who will embrace and follow their Savior. This will happen in a new way of life, in a new time, in this period of history of which Our Lady says is a particular time, an extraordinary time of grace for the world.

CHAPTER EIGHTEEN

The New Way of Life

So is it being written that whatever you do, buy silver? No, the best thing to have is the new way of life Our Lady brings to the world today. Silver can be a means to temporarily help you get there. But on the other hand, silver can be bad if possessed for the wrong reasons. The Bible, in the book of James 5:1–6 shows this danger.

> *"As for you rich, weep and wail over your impending miseries. Your wealth has rotted, your fine wardrobe has grown motheaten, your gold and silver have corroded, and their corrosion shall be a testimony against you; it will devour your flesh like a fire. See what you have stored up for yourselves against the last days. Here, crying aloud, are the wages you withheld from the farmhands who harvested your fields. The cries of the harvesters have reached the ears of the Lord of hosts. You lived in wanton luxury on the earth; you fattened yourselves for the day*

of slaughter. You condemned, even killed, the just man; he does not resist you.."

Christians, for ages, often lined chalices with silver, each destined to hold the Body of Christ. Judas', for ages, have often sold the Body of Christ for 30 pieces of silver, more or less. Both groups have used silver. One group 'lined' the way to Heaven with its proper use. The other 'lined' a slippery slope into hell with its improper use. Therefore, it is not the silver that is good or evil. It is the heart and what is behind your motivation of what you actually carry out. But a word of caution as to intentions of the heart. St. Louis de Montfort said of the evangelizers of the last days who will be the apostles of the last days:

"Attached to nothing... They will sleep without gold or silver..."[83]

Therefore, your intentions in acquiring silver must be based not in love of silver, but love in turning what you have into an instrument of conversion to help all toward an eternal reward. These rounds will be here for generations, who will be 'carrying' the conversion piece. No one will simply throw it away. Your motivation must be first seeking the Kingdom of God, unattached to the hoarding or inordinate want of silver, and for the purpose of what Our Lady's words said:

January 25, 2009

"...for all worldly things to be a help for you to draw you closer to God the Creator..."

It is your actions, that will be judged, not your 'intentions' of what you plan to carry out, because remember the road to hell is also paved with good intentions. Therefore, you must bring into reality efforts for the Kingdom of God. Is your 'silver' for building God's Kingdom and Our Lady's way of life or your kingdom and a worldly way of life?

However, going back in comparing what is the better thing to have: silver and gold or 'a way of life,' the goal is to create a way of life in which you depend less and less on the dollar. In other words, the more you can live well without the need for the dollar, is superior to having silver, gold and the likes. Once you change the direction of your life, and plan to get away from the economic system as it runs today, silver can be used as a transition, a step to help you get to the new way of life that Our Lady is pointing us to. Mary and Joseph being given gold at Jesus' birth, certainly used gold to help them establish a new direction in their lives, when for several years, they had to flee to Egypt. Silver, there-

fore, can be used while you are building a new way of
life, as silver safeguards what you have in the interim,
just as you read in the testimony in chapter nine, in
which the husband and wife spent 12 years sacrificing
and now are secure in their home, by not being laden
with debt or bills. But likewise, Our Lady does not want
you to depend on mammon. When you do, you become
its slave. In that sense, Our Lady does not want you to
seek silver for the sake of silver, for you cannot serve
two masters. Silver is presented to you as what God
made for man, and for you to use it to safeguard what
you have. Paralleling that the use of silver can also help
in Our Lady's plan for conversion, thereby safeguarding
souls.

So what is the way of life? It is the living and earn-
ing your way by God's ordained economic order. The
logic behind it is found in Genesis 3:19:

"By the sweat of your brow shall you eat."

Whether you are very rich, very poor, or in between,
a new way of life, a system of sustenance living is pre-
mium to silver, gold, or money, for the more you depend
on your own resources, the more you are out of debt,
the more you create what God ordained, the more happy you will be. When your life is in harmony with the

principles set forth in the Bible, you are as secure as you possibly can be, spiritually and physically.

Example: you go to the grocery store. You buy four tomatoes for one dollar each. It is priced that high because it is out of growing season for tomatoes. You spent money on gas to go to the store. You pay insurance and maintenance for the car, etc., etc. For insurance, maintenance, expenses, etc., let's ascribe a cost of 25¢ per tomato. While at the grocery store you certainly bought other things, which help lower the ascribed cost of the fuel you spent to go get the tomatoes. So, you spent $4.00 for tomatoes, $1.00 for ascribed costs and 40¢ sales tax. You earned the $5.40 by driving to work each day. Again, more time and effort and more money to add to the cost of your four tomatoes. You do not create any wealth by buying the tomatoes. You lost what you had to pay for them because the whole economic system took from you. It cost you.

In the new way of life of simplicity, Our Lady leads us to, you get one tomato seed, a cost so small that you cannot even ascribe a price to it. You plant it. You nurture it with your labor. You could easily get 30 tomatoes from the one seed of which you use some fresh and the rest you preserve through canning. Your cost could actually be next to nothing, $0.00, and you pay no sales

tax! By doing this, you have created wealth. If you
used 20 tomatoes for canning and used them when out
of season, you generated $20.00 of wealth from noth-
ing but your labor. But one could say, *"That is food and
temporary."* However, apply the same 'wealth creation'
to building your own home and making a pasture, as
the example of the husband and wife who bought the
acre of land for $3,000 and built a comfortable house
for $20,000 — total of $23,000!!! This is generating long
term wealth that will continue working for you with little or no cost. Yes, you will always have property taxes,
but why have taxes, plus debt? While it does take cash
as you create wealth, you can advance yourself and your
family with less and less cash. It is simple.

Instructions: 1. Grow good grass.

                 2. Cow eats grass.

                 3. You eat cow.

These are the principles, however, everybody has forgotten. Growing grass for cows and then milking or
eating them was so important to 'Homeland Security'
that summer was created so children could work the
homestead with the family. It was more important than
pursuing the god of education as it exists now. And the
common sense education children received through

Continue on page 213.

Though we, in the Community of Caritas grow tomatoes in the summertime, in order to can enough to last the entire year, almost the whole community drives an hour away to a local tomato farm at summer's end. We take home with us 100–150 boxes overflowing with tomatoes for an unbelievable low price, one dollar per box!. From there, all the community women and young girls come together each day for a week's worth of canning, with tomatoes literally "coming out of our ears." It's the last "hurrah" of summer. The Community of Caritas cans about 1,200 quarts of tomatoes. Its efforts are as St. Paul relayed, *"Even when I was among you, I worked for my food and keep."* We do the same. Feeding ourselves to be able to give the Caritas mission our labor without burdening the mission to feed us.

Usually a whole day is spent every six months cleaning chickens the community raises. It is a socially joyful time of seeing the fruit of our labor. The agrarian life. This life is not farming, rather the means of a way of life. Work, prayer, and joy lead to a life with meaning, even for the youth who are never given an allowance. They, instead, are given esteem, learn how to work, are self-educated in common sense as their allowance, knowing all the while they are contributing to putting food on the table, a roof over their head, and a world wide mission advancing for conversion to populate Heaven, and where they experience daily a seamless life of Heaven and earth.

working with the family, was packed with learning and far superior to what school's teach today. To start, of course, takes money, but you don't have to do it all at once. And again, as with the husband and wife who built their homestead, it does not take great amounts of money. Initially you must get the land, the home/cottage, etc. And yes, it is better to live around others who are doing the same. "A little chapel surrounded by 4–5 houses — a prophetic vision community."

When one went to Medjugorje in the 1980s, it was wonderful to see the resourcefulness of the village living a sustenance way of life. Many families raised a couple of pigs for the year, smoked them to preserve them without refrigeration, had chickens for eggs and meat, a milk cow, goats, sheep for wool clothing, a small vineyard for wine and a garden for vegetables and fruit. They often did this on less than two acres of land. Living this way brought a high level of freedom from the slavery of the economic order. Medjugorje visionary, Marija, said of her being raised in an agrarian life, that sometimes she remembered crying in the fields because it was hard, but they would come home and stay up until midnight, talking, laughing, cutting up, and just being happy. It was not an idealistic life, rather one of hard work. But they were a happy people, living close to the soil. The main point is they actually created wealth right out of the ground, rather than being only a consumer, in debt and a slave to a serfdom economic system where, in our present system, when people lose their jobs, suddenly they have no way to feed themselves. And as more people lose jobs, the government's capability is limited in giving handouts. How will many be able to eat? This is a serious question to ask yourself. So what happens when the system overloads, as it will do in a paper currency, fiat money system, when wealth is not being created, but rather transferred into the debt balloon, which is only getting bigger? It will pop. Why? Because it can only hold so much air. So what does this mean? It means while we are still limping, bouncing along, waiting for this economy to improve, the balloon is only getting bigger. We are in an urgent time. Use the light of common sense, while you have time, get rid of everything you do not need, downsize, get a little cottage, even a mobile home, get a plot of land. Educate yourself of what is happening around you. **You can go through the door now. When things happen, not everyone is going to be able to squeeze out the door. When the rush is on, it will be too late. The building will collapse, crushing all those still inside, in this case the economy. When it crashes, it will crush everyone to the**

degree they are still tied to the present economic system. Our Lady says use this time well.

October 25, 1985

"...Here you have a time of grace and conversion. It is necessary to use it well."

A time of 'grace' and 'conversion.' It is a grace that Our Lady is showing us a new way of life. And yes, that means to convert and grow in holiness. But it also means we are being given an opportunity to grow in a physical way in a life of holiness, living a way that is close to God the Creator, working with nature, which is like being in church all the time. But nature is not a god as the green movement is idolizing it. Nature is the product of creation, creation is a product of its Creator, the Creator is God, God is 'I Am!' Man has forgotten in his heart from Whom he comes. Therefore, being in nature is a holy place because it is <u>of</u> God, not because it is God.

We know people who have more money than most could imagine, who are getting land and beginning to grow their own food, becoming more independent of the system. All the money in the world cannot get you a can of soup from the grocery store if there is none on the shelf. But love, the labor of love, out of the close-

ness of God in nature can reach up and grab off the
shelf of a cupboard a quart jar of tomatoes you canned
last season, whether you are rich or poor. And it is so
much more gratifying to see the 'fruit' of your hands.
So many women today are out shopping, having lunch
together, doing absolutely foolish stuff, while the hand-
writing is all over the wall. How fond will be the memories of do nothing lives, when one could have spent
years homemaking, building a way of life, a means to
sustain themselves. Saturday sports, the foolish frivoli-
ties of the Saturday all day at the sports 'field' will be a
bitter memory when you realize you could have been in
your own field, building a way of life Our Lady has been
leading us towards.

Our Lady said:

May 2, 2009

"...look at the signs of the times..."

Everyone spends Saturdays having frivolous fun! Our
Lady said:

April 2, 2006

**"...do you not recognize the signs of the times?
Do you not speak of them?..."**

Women frivolously talking to each other, busy being busy, wasting so much valuable and precious time, time spent which will be the cause of caustic bitter lamenting for the time we are coming into. Observe when you are out, for it is self-proving. 'Shop till you drop' will become a true proverb as there will be those dropping to their knees when they come to realize how much time they spent in idleness when they could have channeled those years into building a way of life.

Proverb 12:11

> *"He who tills his own land has food in plenty,*
> *but he who follows idle pursuits is a fool."*

We are in a time of not so much needing to reflect on the past, but rather to reflect on the future that is heading our way like a freight train. Our Lady said:

January 25, 1997

"...I invite you to reflect about your future..."

Our future is Jesus, not mammon. Who is your master? We, at Caritas, have been building Caritas' mission while, at the same time, meeting our life needs through our labor. With one hand evangelizing, and the other hand working to build a 'way of life' as directed by Our Lady. Both hands to build and make Our Lady more known and loved, as St. Louis de Montfort states:

> "...*they will fight with one hand and build with the other. With one hand they will give battle, overthrowing and crushing heretics and their heresies, schismatics and their schisms, idolaters and their idolatries, sinners and their wickedness. With the other hand they will build the temple of the true Solomon and the mystical city of God, namely, the Blessed Virgin...*"[84]

We have spent years not in seeking things, rather in seeking first the Kingdom of God and all these will be given you besides. You must change your direction now. Get out of debt. Take immediate action.

Now, after reading the preceding and being enlightened, decide whether you should put funds into silver. Use the silver transitionally to preserve what you may have, while you find or build yourselves a small homestead, creating a new way of life. Advance by downsizing, then create wealth to upsize. Amish people have a saying:

> "*Many a fine barn built a fine house, but no fine house built a fine barn.*"

In other words, a barn, once built, produces for your well-being. It houses hay that the cow eats. The cow produces milk, etc., until your fine barn produces enough extra to build a fine house. Unlike the cow which eats and produces, a house, when financed, eats mortgage payments, producing little or no advancements, and is like eating all your farm animals before they can produce. You eventually starve, having eaten what was to produce for your future. And many buy or build homes beyond what their true need may be. Their things and house eat far more than a cow! It can eat your whole future's ability to survive. It is why a fine house prevents you from building a fine barn. But a fine barn will eventually allow you to build a modest fine home.

It is important to have no illusions. The above is not a picture perfect life. It requires work, but the saints teach us, work is holy. Today's idleness is sinful and yes, many are very busy doing nothing. It won't be easy to start a new way, but the earthquake that is about to further hit the already broken economy is going to be such that people do not have the imagination to comprehend the depth of the crash because they have no past experiences, nor living memories, with such hardship. Some friends of Caritas from Zimbabwe approached us last year in Medjugorje. They begged for our prayers. They said their fiat paper currency went into hyperinflation overnight, this coupled with bad government officials led people to start turning on each other. All can look at what took place in Greece and other places to understand what began and matured in Zimbabwe. The same can happen anywhere when hyperinflation hits. The following is a news report dated February 11, 2009. This article also shows what people are forced to gravitate back to when fiat currency crashes...precious metal if they can dig for it.

"A film smuggled out of Zimbabwe brings home the economic devastation and deprivation of (their) own people...Sam Chakaipa returned clandestinely to his village, 125 miles from Harare, to document the plight of his former neighbors.

"(It contains)...extraordinary footage of what Zimbabweans have to do in order to survive in a wrecked economy. As money is worthless — Zimbabwe is plagued by the world's highest inflation rate — the villagers are reduced to panning for gold in rivers. Instead of attending school, youngsters from the village scrabble knee-deep in muddy water or dig ever deeper holes in a desperate search for a few grains of gold.

"These small supplies of the precious metal have thus become a crucial commodity Zimbabweans can trade for food; a loaf of bread is worth 0.1 grams. But only the young have the strength to dig and pan for gold; the village elders must go hungry, unless they have friends or relatives they can rely on. Some parents have been forced to feed rats to their children, and hunger has turned family members against each other.

"In a particularly wrenching scene in the video, a 15-year-old girl with a swollen face describes tearfully how her grandmother beat her to drive her away as she was an extra mouth to feed. She says she has not eaten for three days. "I'm hurting all over my body," she says. "There is nothing for me."

"Chakaipa says: 'I have never seen my people in such a desperate situation.' **Nothing is growing in the fields, and the farmers are killing their livestock, effectively destroying their livelihood.**

"...Chakaipa chose to make this film because he wants the world to see what the government, who has been in power since 1980, has done to Zim-

*babwe; how they have reduced a once relatively
prosperous country to ruin"*[85]

'Killing their livestock,' to survive only delays, and
makes certain that starvation is around the corner.
Likewise, the mortgage for the 'fine house' is killing the
ability to get to an agrarian lifestyle that would bring
security such as having livestock and gardening for food
to sustain one's livelihood for the future. Wall Street
says:

"Food is the new gold."[86]

Look across the sea America, look what reckless government officials did to Zimbabwe as we ourselves now
have and peer at our own future. Other nations should
look at Zimbabwe as well.

Greece's perilous financial situation may be followed by Portugal. It is reported that Italy is next in
line for financial failure. Many may become very concerned after reading this chapter. You should. It is
something to be concerned about. Some may be scared
seeing themselves as trapped, in debt, handicapped,
poor, too old to change course, afraid of the future and
of what evil can befall themselves. Whatever your situation, you must remember love is our protection. Our
Lady is love and out of love She comes and says:

February 28, 1985

"...through love you will achieve everything and even what you think is impossible..."

Our Lady knows the future is very dark and something to be afraid of, and there are real valid reasons to be afraid of evil. However, Our Lady said do not be afraid of the future or of evil, and She gave instructions how not to be.

January 25, 2001

"...the one who prays is not afraid of the future and the one who fasts is not afraid of evil..."

This message proves that both a very dark future and fearful evils are coming, but also what to do to conquer the fear of the future and evil. So the legitimate concern after reading this writing should be a motivation to act, not through fear but through concern, and not tomorrow, but yesterday. Our Lady said:

November 2, 2006

"...Your time is a short time..."

Let fear be cast away through prayer. You do not need fear to cloud your decisions. You need hope in a brighter way of life Our Lady is bringing us to. Love will achieve that which you think is impossible. With love, hope fills the heart.

Lastly, tithing ten percent should be seen as one of your highest priorities. Without fulfilling this obligation, with the clear understanding that it is not a suggestion, but a mandate, do not expect God to give you the clarity and a fruitful way of life if you are unwilling to give Him His due.

Six Actions in the Short Time We Have:

1. **Conversion**, then change the direction of your life.

2. Get out of **debt**. Remember Our Lady said, "**...I wish to call you to pray, pray, pray! In prayer you shall perceive the greatest joy and the way out of every situation that has no exit...**" March 28, 1985

3. **Pray** and **fast** for each step, for God to lead you to the new direction. Our Lady said, "**... Do not deceive yourselves that you can do anything without Him** (God)**, not even to take a single step.** September 2, 2006

4. **'Abandon'** all concerns to the Good Father.

5. **Tithe** ten percent of everything you earn. If you
    cannot afford to tithe, it is because you are not
    tithing. No one can afford not to tithe. Life costs
    you more when you do not tithe. It is a Biblical
    mandate. Rich or poor alike. Start now.

6. **Live the sabbath.** If you do not incorporate this
    into your life, forget any hope of rescue. You will
    go down with the rest of the culture. Concerning
    the Sabbath, read the first three chapters of <u>Look
    What Happened While You Were Sleeping</u>_{TM} for
    your personal guidance in following the path
    away from the crash. Read chapters 4-17 for the
    path to save your nation. <u>Look What Happened
    While You Were Sleeping</u>_{TM} is available free as
    an audio book or a printable download book on
    mej.com. Or you can read the first three chap-
    ters online or even the whole book, <u>free</u>.*

---

* On the home page of mej.com, go to the download section on the left-hand side
of the page. Click on books and scroll down to <u>Look What Happened While You
Were Sleeping</u>_{TM}. Click on it and follow the direction to download either the book
or audio, free. You can also buy this important Medjugorje book from Caritas of
Birmingham, Mej Mart, amazon.com, Barnes and Noble, etc.

CHAPTER NINETEEN

**More Astonishing Revelations
About Private Revelations
9 Questions**

Answers that will Astound You

1. What does the image on the back of the Miraculous Medal tell us?

2. Aside from the Two Hearts, is the rest of the image on back just a trendy design?

3. Did St. Catherine understand all the meaning?

4. Is it possible that Our Lady did not explain the detail because it was more for the future than the present?

5. Could anyone truly understand if the image had a prophetic nature, until it came of age?

6. Is now the time the mysteries in the medal are to be revealed?

7. In looking on the back of the Miraculous Medal, of course, one could explain the cross being a symbol of salvation, the Sacred and Immaculate Hearts, the 12 stars, but until now, could anyone, without deep prayer, understand the full image?

8. Are we to think the shape and thickness of the lines forming the image do not have a special purpose to speak to us, that past generations could not understand as prophetic because it makes no sense until fulfilled?

9. As Our Lady said you must pray to comprehend Her messages, should it not be the same to reveal the prophetic nature on the back of the Miraculous Medal?

This is Our Lady's time. Now is the time for all these questions to be answered for our age. The answers to the questions, however, won't be given one by one as in the above format, but rather they will be answered in the general discussion that follows within the pages of this chapter. Our Lady wants to reveal these things to praying hearts, so we can understand the true reason for Her coming. Our Lady said:

June 25, 1991

"...If you pray, God will help you discover the true reason for my coming..."

This chapter is derived through much prayer, for you to learn that prayer can help you discover what is in front of you and yet you cannot see. The answers to the nine questions at the beginning of this chapter may surprise you! But first, you must understand the background surrounding St. Catherine before discovering what the back of the Miraculous Medal reveals prophetically. Again, what follows is to enlighten you in order to grasp the significance of the answers to the nine questions.

Except for her confessor, Fr. Aladel, the bishop, and in later years, only one or two others, no one knew St. Catherine was the one who received from Our Lady the apparition image of the Miraculous Medal. St. Catherine lived in her convent, so unassumingly as a visionary, that no one through the decades knew she was the visionary who received the Miraculous Medal! Yet she said her whole life was one of martyrdom. Why? Because of her superiors. It took St. Catherine two years to finally get her confessor to have the Miraculous Medal struck. He had repeatedly silenced Catherine from even talking about it, until one day when he addressed her, she responded the Blessed Mother was angry with him. Catherine, after the original three apparitions, was receiving instructions from Our Lady through inner locutions. The French Marian theologian, Rene Laurentin, writes:

> "What should she do when faced with these contradictory instructions from Our Lady on the one hand and God's representative on the other? In the autumn, she summoned up the courage to reply to Our Lady: 'He, Fr. Aladel, does not want to listen to me." **'He is my servant,' answered the voice inside her, 'and he should be frightened of displeasing me.'** Catherine tried again to get through a third time to him on Our Lady's account. **'The Virgin is angry,'** she brought herself to say. Fr. Aladel remained like marble; but these words affected him and tormented him in his turn. Could he be a 'bad servant' of 'Her whom he loved to call, 'Refuge of Sinners?'"[87]

That Our Lady was upset with him, stunned Fr. Aladel. After contemplating these words of Sr. Catherine, he went to the bishop who told Fr. Aladel to have the image struck and to give it out without explanation. As distribution began, many people came back for more, claiming miracles associated with the medals. Soon millions were distributed while the people kept coming to the convent, wanting what they themselves termed as the 'miracle' medal. However, what no one knew or realized was the continued agony of St. Catherine who was being instructed by Our Lady to seek from her superiors to have the chapel of the Miraculous Medal open for pilgrimages. St. Catherine's superiors repeatedly rejected the notion. Our Lady had pronounced to Catherine that when Church authorities would do this, countless miracles would be granted, just as what was happening with the Miraculous Medal. Our Lady's directive to open the chapel was a second part of a three part plan of conversion, originally inaugurated with the Miraculous Medal. The superiors refused to open the chapel. This was a most difficult task for Catherine, as Our Lady several times had told her to tell her superiors that the opening of the chapel where Our Lady gave the Miraculous Medal to pilgrimages was Her wish and there would be great graces and blessings bestowed upon Catherine's community when this was accomplished. The Chapel on Rue du Bac would be a place of miracles, just as the Miraculous Medal had millions of miracles associated with it. For 34 agonizing years, St. Catherine's request was rejected in regards to what Our Lady wanted, even though the confessor knew and believed Our Lady appeared to her.

But what is amazing is what St. Catherine tells us in regards to this refusal. After 28 years, in which Rue du Bac had not been opened because of Catherine's superiors, Our Lady then appeared elsewhere! Catherine, herself, confirmed that the graces being given at Lourdes, in France, through the visionary Bernadette, were supposed to have happened in the Miraculous Medal Chapel of Catherine's community.

> *"According to Sr. Tranchemer, her companion, Catherine said, 'You know, these miracles could have happened in our chapel.' Apparently she said the same to Sr. Millon: 'If the superiors had wanted it, the Blessed Virgin would have chosen our chapel.'"*[88]

After Catherine's death, it was revealed to all that she was the visionary and that she confirmed, she even told Our Lady to go on and appear elsewhere.

> *" According to Sr. Pineau, Sr. Dufes found in Catherine's belongings a piece of paper; on it were written these words in the sister's own hand: 'My*

kind Mother, here no one wants to do what you want; manifest yourself somewhere else![89]

"When Catherine heard people talking about the Lourdes apparition (1858), she said, 'It's the same one!' 'What is most extraordinary,' wrote Sr. Dufes, her superior, 'is that, without having read any of the published works, Sr. Catherine was more conversant with what had taken place [in Lourdes] *there than those who had actually made this pilgrimage.'"*[90]

The apparitions of Lourdes were outside the 'permission needed' by Church authorities, superiors and politics! Our Lady appeared outdoors in the open to Bernadette in Lourdes. The apparitions happened as lightning where an okay was not needed and free from man's misjudgments of which excess caution and politics caused Catherine martyrdom through her vow of obedience. This vow for Catherine is something of which we all, as members of the universal Church are bound by, according to our state, religious or laity, according to Church jurisdiction. However, by rite/right of baptism, everyone is commissioned to evangelize Christianity. One does not need permission. One is obligated to evangelize.

When the apostles complained there were people who were spreading His teaching even though they were not connected to any of the apostolic group Jesus had selected, Jesus responded:

"He that is not against you is for you," Luke 9:50

Therefore, one does not need permission to evangelize. This freedom to evangelize, however, does not apply to heretical teachings or private revelations condemned. In that case, the Church has full jurisdiction to rule over all, not only Catholics but even other denominations as well. A bishop is bishop over everyone in a diocese, both, all Christians and non-believers. It is not dependent upon if the people grant the bishop this authority, for it comes from God not man. But, at the same time, the Church membership is granted authority by God, through baptism, to be evangelizers. One does not need permission from a bishop. One is commissioned automatically as a baptized Christian as long as there is the absence of heresy or absence of condemnation of the devotion, message, etc. <u>Our Lady Queen of Peace of Medjugorje wants us to especially understand this freedom and liberty God has granted and commissioned us with.</u> *"He that is not against you is for you."* It is of primary importance to understand this for Her plans to succeed. Through Medjugorje, the whole world will come to salvation, and the laity must not be stopped in their effort to evangelize the messages. Our Lady wants you to clearly understand that it is She who calls you. It is She who commissions you, because God has granted the authority to you through baptism. However, Catherine's dilemma, as well as the Holy Virgin Mary's was that <u>both</u> were under the direct jurisdiction of the superiors, through Catherine's vow of obedience. She always complied with this, and she taught the other novices under her care to do the same. The lesson learned here, however, is why Our Lady went to Lourdes and how Heaven's plans can be stymied, even stopped by the ministers charged with the propagation of the faith.

Catherine, when hearing of the wonderful stories of the miracles taking place at Lourdes felt more keenly her ongoing martyrdom due to her superiors continual rejection of Our Lady's pleas. Catherine's torment was a *great joy lost* because of the refusal of her superiors to open their chapel, and the fact that what happened in Lourdes would have happened in their own convent's chapel. In Rene Laurentin's work, <u>Catherine Laboure</u>, it is stated:

> "'On *different occasions,' Sr. Cosnard tells us, 'Sr. Catherine went to* **great lengths** *to persuade me*

*that the pilgrimage of Notre Dame des Victoires, whose Association wore the Miraculous Medal, and the Lourdes pilgrimage had been <u>granted by the Blessed Virgin in order to '**compensate**'</u> for those that the superiors had not seen it necessary to authorize via our chapel.'"*[91]

While Catherine was hearing the voice of Our Lady, the voices of her superiors contradicted Our Lady's request. Yet, they had evidence of the fruits of the Miraculous Medal. Rene Laurentin writes:

"The torture of not being listened to made Catherine a little stiff and tense at certain times."[92]

Catherine continued to feel sorry that the chapel at Rue du Bac was not open to pilgrims, for she was still being urged by Our Lady's promise that:

"'People will know where I have been.'...Catherine would sigh when hearing about the cure of a deaf-mute at Lourdes and say, 'You know, all these miracles should have taken place in our chapel.'"[93]

Rene Laurentin writes:

"Catherine was also still very concerned about the Rue du Bac — an unrecognized fountain (of

grace) sealed-off (the fountain or spring miracles that were now granted in Lourdes).[94]

Catherine continues:

'The pilgrimage that the sisters (of St. Catherine's order) *make to other places are not helpful to their piety. The Blessed Virgin did not say that you had to go and pray so far away. It's in the chapel of the community that She wants the sisters to invoke Her. There (in the chapel) is THEIR pilgrimage.'*[95]

We now know, as Laurentin writes:

"Catherine is also credited with supernatural intuitions regarding the distribution of the medal, as well as the rapid launching of Lourdes…and she saw influxes of pilgrims **'compensating'** *for those who could not go to the Rue du Bac, since the decision to open it had not been taken."*[96]

It is an amazing revelation to learn Lourdes and its miracles were supposed to be at Rue du Bac and that Our Lady was rejected and the *plan of pilgrimage* Our Lady wanted, had turned to Lourdes to dispense the grace which God had already granted Her but which man would not.

After Catherine's death, the chapel was finally opened, but the miracles and countless conversion that were to be, were now owned by Lourdes. And yet still, another martyrdom for Catherine involved a statue of Our Lady holding the globe. It was to be placed in the Rue du Bac chapel, on the spot the apparition took place. Yet, this too was rejected. Laurentin writes of Catherine revealing Our Lady's request to a sister, in a hidden way:

> *"Sr. Cosnard knew about sharing things on a deep level (with Catherine). In this way, she managed to get Catherine to talk about the apparitions by means of large hints without Catherine having to reveal herself. Thus Catherine was able to confide in her the message which was so close to her heart."*[97]

Catherine told Sr. Cosnard:

> *'When she appeared to one of our sisters...the Most Holy Virgin held a globe of the world in her hands. She was offering it...No engraving of the apparitions portrays her like this. But she wants it and she wants an altar on the spot where She appeared.'"*[98]

Laurentin writes:

*"Too many obstacles had bruised her, too many
refusals had torn her between obedience to the
Virgin, whose messenger she was, and obedience
to the confessors who rejected her requests. Her
conscience had suffered violently."[99]*

Catherine's request, on behalf of Our Lady, to have a
statue of Our Lady, holding a globe, sculpted was rejected by her confessor because he said it would confuse
people with the image already struck on the medal.
Catherine responded to her superior:

*"Oh, there is no need to touch the Miraculous
Medal!"[100]*

However, from 1839 on, Fr. Aladel refused. Catherine
responded in regard to her Sr. superior:

*"'It was my martyrdom of my life,' admitted
Catherine, who could not resign herself to the
omission."[101]* *

All the above again is to enlighten you step by step
to understand in simplicity the whole of the back of
the Miraculous Medal. Knowing what Catherine went

---

* The statue of Our Lady holding the globe, marking the spot of the apparitions,
  was finally placed in the chapel four years after Catherine's death.

through helps one understand. With Our Lady giving the Miraculous medal, a three part plan for conversion is realized:

FIRST: The medal itself for conversion.

SECOND: Connected with giving the medal was pilgrimages to the chapel for conversion. This was denied and, therefore, Lourdes was given in compensation.

THIRD;   What is the third part of the conversion plan of Our Lady?

Catherine had presented another major third part of Our Lady's plan shown on the back of the medal, which remarkably was yet again rejected by her superiors. Our Lady wanted something very special instituted in France, not just for France and their conversion, but for the conversion of people who would *come from all over the world.* Rejected by her superiors, this wish of Our Lady was not fulfilled.

Laurentin tells the story. Catherine, during the revolution of 1848, when hearing that when some rebel went to ransack Tuileries, a young man, fearing sacrilege, ran to the chapel to take away sacred vessels and the crucifix. The virtuous young man held up the crucifix, shouting, "Long Live the Christ!" When the rebel began angrily yelling back at him, the young man held the Crucifix, even higher into the air and shouted, "You want new life? Well, don't forget you can only have it through Christ." "Yes! Yes!" they replied back, throwing hats up, shouting back, "Long Live the Christ."[102] This change of spirit of the crowd at the sight of the cross, sparked in Catherine the remembrance of a yet unfulfilled directive — the third part of the plan of conversion. When Catherine heard of the angry crowd against the young man who responded by holding the cross higher, she reminisced Our Lady's third directive, in regard to the Cross, that would challenge the people to conversion, once the Cross was held high in front of them. Catherine relayed:

> *"… a vision suddenly and freely took place within her, as previously: what was given to her was the triumph of the cross, a triumph that had to be BROUGHT TO LIFE. A monumental crucifix must be erected in Paris. It would strengthen the bonds between Christians and Christ crucified."[103]*

Catherine had been told by Our Lady that She, Our Lady, wanted a cross to be erected in front of Notre Dame. Catherine described what Our Lady told her.

'This cross will be called the cross of victory. It will be the object of much veneration. From all over France and from countries further away, even from overseas, some will come because of devotion, others on pilgrimage, and still others through simple curiosity. And, of course, special protections will occur that will be thought miraculous. Not a single person will come to Paris and not come to see and visit this cross as if it were a work of art.'[104]

Catherine described the size of the cross:

"The foot of the cross seemed to me to be 10 to 12 feet square and the cross itself from 15 to 20 feet high. Once erected, it appeared to me to be about 30 feet high."[105]

Laurentin:

"This lifelike vision was full of hope. Catherine felt impelled to present it to Fr. Aladel. 'Here we go again!' he thought and reiterated his stereotype advice against illusions. Catherine tried again — in vain. She therefore decided to take up her pen on July 30, 1848.

'Father, this is...the third time that I have spoken to you about this cross.'"[106]

Yet, it was rejected. According to Rene Laurentin:

"... and if the cross she (Catherine) *had asked for had been erected, there could have been a rapid expansion* (conversion and miracles) *like that of the Miraculous Medal. This movement would have been the logical **crowning point of her visions** — it would have re-centered them on Christ. Catherine was deeply impregnated by this logic. She expressed it in one of her last utterances when, on her deathbed..."[107]*

In <u>Catherine Laboure</u>, Laurentin's book, he sums up the unrealized predictions of Catherine:

"The symbolic vision of a cross set up in the square in front of Notre Dame has been denounced... But here it is less a case of an unrealized prediction than a request that was refused...If Catherine's cross had been realized, it would doubtless have produced a wave of devotion and grace similar to that produced by the Miraculous medal. It would have been a Christological complement to and a crowning of the message, in the sense of that which

is at the summit of the message: the cross which dominates the Miraculous medal."[108]

So Our Lady's three part conversion plan:

1. For the conversion of individuals—the Miraculous Medal.

2. For the conversion, particularly of France—pilgrims to the chapel.

3. For the conversion of those who would come to the Cross and also from foreign countries—a Cross to be erected in front of Notre Dame.

As it turned out, only the first part did not have to be compensated for. The second part of the conversion plan was compensated through Lourdes becoming the place for pilgrimages when the superiors refused to open the Chapel at Rue du Bac. And the third?

1. Miraculous Medal realized millions of conversions and miracles.

2. Pilgrimage to Rue du Bac's chapel, as an apparition site in which millions of miracles and cures and conversions would have occurred, instead was rejected. Our Lady still granted this grace, transferring it to Lourdes.

3. A Cross erected in front of Notre Dame for the whole world to come to was rejected and never realized. Yet, it dominates the back of the Miraculous Medal, the third part of the plan of conversion.

Why didn't Our Lady compensate for the third part of Her plan, the cross, establishing it somewhere else so people from all over the world could come to it, just as She had compensated for the second part of Her plan, which when the refusal of pilgrimages to Rue du Bac resulted in Our Lady granting Lourdes?

Most are well aware of the meaning of the Sacred Heart and Immaculate Heart, the twelve stars. But what of the rest of the medal? Is there a prophetic nature yet to be understood?

Why would Our Lady give an image on the back of a medal with some distinct varying details if She did not wish to speak to the people through it? Otherwise, it would just be a trendy design, something we know Our Lady would not do. Our Lady speaks, not in theologi-

cally complex ways, but in simple ways. Jesus spoke also
in this way, so simple; the same way Our Lady speaks, so
simple in Her messages. The same way Claude Newman
surpassed all theological explanations of the Real Presence when he said:

> *"She (Our Lady) told me that in Communion I*
> *will only see what looks like a piece of bread. But*
> *She told me that that is really and truly Her Son*
> *and that He will be with me just for a few mo-*
> *ments as He was with Her before He was born in*
> *Bethlehem. She told me that I should spend my*
> *time like She did in all Her time with Him, by lov-*
> *ing Him, adoring Him, thanking Him, praising*
> *Him and asking Him for the blessings. I shouldn't*
> *be bothered by anybody else or anything else.*
> *And I should spend my two or three minutes with*
> *Him."* [109]

What else does one need to believe about the Real
Presence except simple childlike faith and belief? Likewise, Our Lady wishes, in a simple way, to reveal to you
what, to this point, has been hidden for 180 years. It is
now revealed as Our Lady revealed to Claude so simply
the explanation of the Eucharist.

Enlightened about Our Lady's request to Catherine for plans of conversion, of which the medal's purpose was to make Our Lady more known and loved, you can now understand the following.

The Miraculous Medal's Prophetic Nature Revealed.

One cannot suppose the bars that make up the letter 'M' on the back of the Miraculous Medal, all with different thickness in 'M' and other symbols is not without a message. What is that message?

'I'mmaculate

Our Lady is the 'I'mmaculate One. The only one worthy enough to make the last call for the end times to prepare us before Jesus' second coming. The 'I' is clearly distinguished apart from the 'M', to signify what the meaning of the medal is: "O Mary, conceived without sin." 'I'mmaculate.

The first leg thick and the second thin, a clear '**V**' is distinguished in the image as clearly lifting off from the '**M**', and stands apart distinctly for '**V**'irgin

A clear '**M**' for Mary

It cannot be without intended purpose that Our Lady gave the image on the Miraculous Medal in 1830, and that 24 years later, on December 8, 1854, Pius IX defined the Dogma of the Immaculate Conception. The medal had been prophetic.

'I'mmaculate 'V'irgin 'M'ary

The revelation of the 'M' shows how simply Our Lady gives meaning just as the messages in Medjugorje are given. It is the same way Jesus taught His truths, not seen or comprehended until simple prayer finds what is there all along.

So why was the second part of the plan shifted to Lourdes as compensation for Rue du Bac's rejection as a place of pilgrimage, but the third part of the plan of conversion had no compensation? Our Lady did not get Her Cross in Paris. She got it somewhere else. Now you can begin to understand, but that is because it is being explained to you. It was revealed through prayer, and though you can understand by these words, you cannot comprehend without prayer the significance of the prophetic nature of Our Lady putting the Cross on the Miraculous Medal. It is the same with Our Lady's messages. You can read Her words, but cannot understand their full significance without prayer. Our Lady said on October 25, 1988:

"...pray that you may comprehend the greatness of this message which I am giving you..."

You must pray if you want to comprehend the spiritual trail Our Lady is leaving and why. Because, yes, Our Lady did get Her Cross! And along with that Cross, She got a Mountain, Mt. Križevac, known to millions as Cross Mountain in Medjugorje! And people come from foreign countries to it. The whole world comes to this Cross and millions of miracles of conversion and spiritual healing have occurred there, just as with the first stage of the plan, the **Miraculous Medal**, the second, the place of pilgrimage in **Lourdes** and now the third part of Our Lady's plan of salvation — **the Cross** in Medjugorje. Doesn't it seem odd that included in the image of the Cross is a base that threads through the '**M**' on the Miraculous Medal? The base of the Cross shown would not traditionally be on or seen with an image of the Cross. This is not a trendy design. The

Cross, with the base, would not be there if Our Lady wasn't prophetic in seeing to the future. For, what was rejected in Paris would be compensated for by a Cross that now most amazingly matches the dimensions Catherine described! The Cross on Cross Mountain in Medjugorje stands approximately 30' tall, with a base of about 10' wide! Incredibly, Catherine gave dimensionally, from what she saw in a vision, nearly exactly the size of the Cross which ended up being built in Medjugorje! Catherine said:

> *"The foot of the Cross seemed to me to be 10 to 12 feet square and the Cross itself from 15 to 20 feet high. Once erected, it appeared to me to be about 30 feet high"*[110]

St. Catherine was good at dimensions. She took care of all the animals in her community and had a meticulous reputation for her accuracy in accounting for the number of eggs the chickens would lay, even thousands of eggs through the years under her practical judgement. The accuracy of what St. Catherine estimated the size of the Cross she saw in a vision and how it matches the size of the Cross on Cross Mountain in Medjugorje is more than amazing.

Be filled with joy as you meditate on the image. Enjoy a surreal state if you have had the gift of climbing that mountain and prayed under that prophetic Cross that was rejected by Catherine's superiors. But this cross was accepted by the people because it was already set as a compensation in Our Lady's plans before it was even built, compensation for what could have, what would have happened in Paris — millions of conversions from everywhere. Need the Medjugorje connection? Read the incredible connection of Our Lady's words. Our Lady said:

August 31, 1984

> **"I love the cross which you have <u>providentially</u> erected on Mount Križevac in a very special way. Go there more often and pray."**

Astounding! **"…which you have 'providentially' erected…in a special way…"** Our Lady said:

March 18, 1996

> **"…Do not reject from yourself the name of God, that you may not be rejected. Accept my messages that you may be accepted…"**

The special Cross in Medjugorje that the whole world is coming to, giving millions of conversions. Our Lady said a most profound Biblical statement while appearing to the visionaries on this mountain with thousands present. Our Lady said:

June 24, 1986

> **"You are on a Tabor…"**

Along with the second plan of conversion being rejected and then compensated for, the third is now standing
on Cross Mountain, built by peasant villagers, as what
was to be in Paris was rejected. Our Lady tells us more
about the Cross, providentially built in Medjugorje as
part of Her conversion plan.

December 31, 1981

> **"…Almost everyday I am at the foot of the Cross.**
> **My Son carried the Cross. He has suffered on the**
> **Cross, and by it, He saved the world. Everyday I**
> **pray to my Son to forgive the sins of the world."**

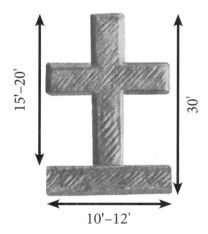

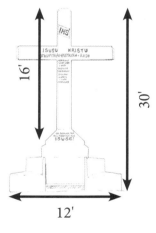

Miraculous Medal Cross prophetically foretold on the back
of the medal and the dimensions
Catherine saw in the vision as
the size "seemed" to her: a cross
15'–20' tall, base 10'–12' square,
when standing a total of 30' in all.

The Cross rejected by Sr. Catherine's
superiors, now stands on Cross Mountain in Medjugorje built to dimensions
above in compensation. Amazing
dimensions of what Sr. Catherine saw:
The Medjugorje cross measuring, 16'
tall, base 12' square, and when standing 30' in all.

If one never had the chance to go to Medjugorje, get
a Miraculous Medal. Meditate on all these wondrous
things Our Lady is revealing through prayer in our time
and go there in your heart. Where is there?

Prophetically again, Our Lady says where.

'M'EDJUGORJE

The key to begin seeing what you cannot see.

Prayer, Peace, Fasting, and Penance

You do these things and you will be able to begin to
see into the future. You will know what decisions to
make. You can perceive what God has blessed you
with and you can use the same for the salvation of
those who carry the **Miraculous Medal Medjugorje Silver Round**.

This writing is a letter to all who love Our Lady and those who will fall in love with Her in the future and want to make Her more known and loved. The revelations you have read should not only astound you and be a cause of joy, but also a motivation to put into action what you now know. We must regain our power of discernment. Remember, Our Lady said:

May 2, 2009

"...You are permitting sin to overcome you more and more. You are permitting it to master you and to take away your power of discernment..."

Remember Our Lady's words:

November 2, 2006

"...Your time is a short time..."

Incorporate the November 27, 1989 Miraculous Medal Medjugorje message into life, spreading devotion, conversion, and the changes that come through living Our Lady's messages in order that the Claude Newmans,

A Friend of Medjugorje was given the understanding about the meaning of the of back of the Miraculous Medal before he began this book or read any details about St. Catherine. He initially had nothing to back the discernment, inspiration, and understanding he received through prayer. As he began his research for It Ain't Gonna Happen™, he began to find material that actually confirmed the understanding he received of the multi-meaning of the back of the Miraculous Medal.

through your witness and by God's grace, will convert. It will be necessary with this writing, as is often the case with Our Lady's messages, to immediately start re-reading it. It will give you just as much in the second read and even more than your first read. Read later a second, third, fourth time and more. It will reveal more through the Holy Spirit every time you read it. Buy at least 10 copies and give them away. The messages are so important to spread in the short time we have that we are pricing the book less than the cost of production so that you can buy in volume of 10, 50, 100 500, even 1000 copies for your whole parish. See page 270 for volume pricing. It will transform all who are open to the light of Jesus' common sense as Our Lady said He is:

December 2, 2007

"...the light of common sense."

You are billboards for what has been illuminated in this 'letter' to you. Spread this writing and, yes, spread the devotion and the carrying of the Miraculous Medal Medjugorje Silver Round. Millions of conversions can result from your efforts. Begin serious prayer. The Holy Spirit will inspire you to steps and decisions Our Lady wants you to take.

As to acquiring the Miraculous Medal Medjugorje Silver Round for transitional purposes, as you build your new way of life, for preserving and safeguarding what you have acquired or to give for baptism, wedding, First Communion gifts, etc. or just to evangelize, information follows at the end of this chapter.

For those who continue to cling to the hope the economic order will recover, or that your equity in your home will stabilize or grow, your stock investments will be secure, your savings will keep its value, your assets will appreciate and life, as we've known it, will continue and things will return as the past years...

It ain't gonna happen...

In the Love of Our Lady and
Praying for You to Gain
the Power of Discernment,

A Friend of Medjugorje

P.S. Warning: do not buy silver without physically holding silver. Buying silver and holding paper certificates is too risky. The silver that is held in reserve for you may have several obligations for the same silver. For example, if you buy 100 oz. physical silver on paper, the current market may hold only one ounce. If you want your 100 ounces today, you could obtain them because many ounces of silver are there in reserve for many people. But, what if everyone wants their silver at the same time? If everyone rushes to cash in their paper holdings to silver, it's not going to be there. That is another reason the Miraculous Medal Medjugorje Round is physically placed in your possession. <u>Do not buy</u> physical silver held in paper transactions.

The Miraculous Medal Medjugorje Round is available two ways. Caritas is a mission. Our life's purpose is working for conversions and the world's salvation. We, therefore, are not in the silver business. Instead of physical silver, our silver 'is' the new way of life Our Lady has shown us and led us to for well over 25 years in the making. This way of life was inspired and discerned even before Our Lady appeared in 1981.

The Miraculous Medal Medjugorje Rounds have now been minted officially as of **6/24**/10 and available two ways.

1.   You can go to mej.com or call Caritas for your convenience on ordering smaller amounts of 1-50 rounds or to acquire the Miraculous Medal Medjugorje Rounds on a weekly basis or another

timetable. Caritas does not hold any silver in inventory nor does Caritas ship your rounds. They will be drop shipped to you directly. Again this is offered only as a convenience for you. For more ordering information, you may call Caritas of Birmingham at 205-672-2000 or go online to http://www.medjugorje.com/silver-round.html.

2. For large quantities to transfer savings or to hold your cash in silver, transfer retirements, stocks, and transfer your investments into silver and/or to hold transitionally while you build a new way of life and for any questions you may have or need to discuss, you can contact **globalsilverinvestors.com** or email at **globalsilverinvestors@yahoo.com.** You can also call Global Silver Investors at 1-877-93M-ROUND or 1-877-936-7686.

Caritas is not connected to globalsilverinvestors.com. We have allowed them to use our design of the Miraculous Medal Medjugorje Round in order to distribute them inexpensively as close to spot price as possible.

How much does the one ounce Miraculous Medal Medjugorje Round cost? Very little compared to specialty silver rounds which typically go for several dollars over spot. 'Spot price' is the worldwide price of silver at the moment you buy silver.

Three to five dollars or more over spot **will not** be the case for the Miraculous Medal Medjugorje Rounds. The cost of minting one Miraculous Medal Medjugorje Round will be well below most any other way to buy one ounce rounds of .999 pure silver. This inexpensive price is to help you and to help souls to be led to conversion by getting wider distribution. Therefore, the Miraculous Medal Medjugorje Round for one troy ounce .999 silver will be approximately $1.25 over worldwide spot price. Again, this spot price per ounce of silver depends on market conditions. You must contact **globalsilverinvestors.com** to get daily pricing. The ability to exchange currency for one ounce rounds so cheaply is due to giving you wholesale mint prices through large volume pricing. This is because the goal is not to sell silver, but rather to get the Miraculous Medal Medjugorje Round out into the culture. Even if one holds it for a lifetime, it will eventually spread out to Our Lady's children, believers and non-believers, both of whom need conversion.

Even before the official release of the Miraculous Medal Medjugorje Rounds, several people we know transferred a portion or all their holdings into the rounds, already totalling 47,905 rounds which is equivalent to over **one million dollars** into the Miraculous Medal Medjugorje Silver Rounds. The official release was the **6/24**/2010 date. It must be stated clearly: We do not represent professional financial advice. Everything written concerns handling financial decisions from a Biblical perspective or through Our Lady's messages. Caritas of Birmingham, the Community of Caritas, the author a Friend of Medjugorje, and any associates or others who are not part of Caritas such as globalsilverinvestors.com or 3M Distributions LLC, are not responsible for any losses in any way as to how you use the information found in this work or any information transferred to you by phone, mail, and any other means of communication. You are responsible for your own decisions independent of what is stated or transmitted to you in any way, shape, fashion, or form.

Questions

The following is from a talk given on July 5, 2010 on location at Caritas, after the release of It Ain't Gonna Happen™. The following questions were asked to a Friend of Medjugorje and Frank Francis of Global Silver Investors by those gathered for the July 1-5 Prayer Gathering for the Re-consecration of the United States of America. A suggestion was made to include these answers in the book to further clarify how the silver rounds would be distributed.

Question: *How long will it take to receive the Miraculous Medal Medjugorje Rounds from the time you order them until the time they're received?*

Frank: The rounds are not made ahead of time. Global Investors or Caritas do not store anything. These Miraculous Medal Medjugorje Rounds are not being made available for the purpose of making a profit. It is a ministry to us. It's more about getting the Miraculous Medals out in circulation and for whatever Our Lady wants to do in the future. What happens is you will either wire your funds or send a check for the amount of silver you want to purchase. When the money has cleared, Global Silver Investors will purchase the silver and then whatever mint that we're using, we'll have the silver delivered to them. When the mint gets it, they'll stamp the Miraculous Medal Medjugorje Round image on the round for us and then generally it should be about three week's delivery time to your home. It could be sooner than that. It depends on a lot of things, but it shouldn't take more than three weeks from the time your funds are cleared.

Question: *Is there a minimum order?*

Frank: There is no minimum order as far as quantity goes. We receive a quantity discount from the mint when we order in volumes of 500 ounces or more. But as we'll be getting orders in everyday, we will be able to combine the orders to reach that 500 minimum for the special pricing. Within a day or two, we will be able to put these orders together, and again, we anticipate that once payment has cleared, we are looking at approximately three weeks before delivery.

Question: *Who is Global Silver Investors and what is Caritas' role in all of this?*

Answer by A Friend of Medjugorje: This is a good question because Frank and Global Silver Investors are completely separate from Caritas of Birmingham. What Frank is doing, he is doing. Caritas of Birmingham is not the broker for the round, nor does it have any financial vested interest in this. Our concern is that we are the conversion side of this spiritual project. As a community, we are accommodating, seeking, and propagating through Our Lady's messages spiritual wealth. From the Caritas side of the fence, the round was designed and worked to negotiate the best cost, whittling it down further and further to get the lowest possible cost to mint the image. Global Silver Investors organization is who handles the ordering and shipping of the Miraculous Medal Medjugorje Rounds. Anything else Caritas does is for your convenience and to promote the image and why to do so, especially through It Ain't Gonna Happen_{TM}.

Question: *What would we normally pay for pure silver rounds?*

Frank: You can't buy any silver round at this cost ($1.25 above spot) that is anywhere near the same quality of the Miraculous Medal Medjugorje rounds. Any other specialty round like this goes for at least $3 or more above spot but without anything near the quality. You can get a silver round at a similar cost, but not anything as beautiful or high quality as the Miraculous Medal Round, or with the dual purpose of conversion of souls.

Question: *We have been told that there are already some miraculous happenings in regards to the Miraculous Medal Medjugorje rounds?*

Frank: I guess the first miracles would be a personal one in regards to a tornado that came through my own property in June, 2010. I had a few silver rounds I traded for the Miraculous Medal Medjugorje rounds to personally have for each one of my family members. Shortly after receiving them, a very damaging tornado whipped through my neighborhood. The house on the east side of my own house was destroyed by a huge tree falling down upon it and the barn on the west side of me came apart like a house of cards. Debris was everywhere, like a war zone. Though my house suffered minimal damage from the flying shrapnel, my property was basically untouched, while being surrounded by complete devastation. Not even our chicken coop was touched or damaged. It was still standing there, unharmed. I attribute all that to Our Lady's protection.

Something else extraordinary happened with a friend of mine. His name is Kurt. He lives off his social security income. He has a disability, and basically during the day he roams the streets as a pedestrian in the city where he lives. He is a Protestant, but not one who practices his faith or goes to church. He's not really religiously affiliated to any church. He's been walking the streets in this city for 30 years—his way of passing the time. I hadn't seen him in a long time. Usually he will call me around the time of his birthday each year, reminding me of his birthday, and I'll buy him some clothes and take him out to lunch. It was Father's Day weekend and I was visiting my Dad in my home town where I was born. Kurt ended up calling me, and I had already planned on going over and seeing him. For his birthday, after taking him out for lunch, I gave him a one-ounce Miraculous Medal Medjugorje round as a gift, giving him a brief explanation of Our Lady and the specialty round. I then dropped him off at a nearby store.

The next day, his friend that I had just met the day before called me and said, "Kurt is in the hospital. He was run over by a car!" I asked, "How bad is it?" I was told that Kurt had broke his neck, but they didn't know if he was paralyzed from it or if he had suffered permanent damage. I asked if Kurt was in a coma. His friend told me, "No, he can talk." That was on a Sunday. I told him that I would go visit Kurt in the hospital the next day. By Monday, Kurt was already walking. He had a halo on, with two places broken in his neck. When he saw me, he began to cry telling me, *"Your Lady saved me."* I call the Blessed Mother 'Our Lady', so he referred to Her as 'Your Lady.' (laughter) But he said, *"She saved my life."* He was crying. He said, *"I'd be dead if it weren't for Her."*

Kurt wasn't a believer in this, but he believes now. So, these are just some of the beautiful things we're bound to see more of in the future. Because first of all, grace comes as the result of your intention for seeing this Miraculous Medal round spread. What is your intention for doing this? The first has to be conversion. That is our motivation.

* * * * * * * * * *

Because the above stories and miracles are of inter-
est to everyone, please send in any testimonies or sto-
ries that you have experienced through the Miraculous
Medal Medjugorje Rounds. Send your testimonies to
Caritas of Birmingham, 100 Our Lady Queen of Peace
Drive, Sterrett, Alabama 35147.

RadioWAVE™
Mejanomics

Every Thursday
LIVE on mej.com

Placing Our Lady's Messages as a
Template Over Your Financial Problems

On November 19, 2009, the first *Mejanomics* show aired on Medjugorje.com, Caritas of Birmingham's website. It was added to the radio programming of *RadioWAVE*™, with the host, A Friend of Medjugorje.

Since the 1980s, a Friend of Medjugorje was inspired to use a concept of applying Our Lady's messages not only to what most think, such as prayer, fasting, etc., but all things of life and culture on earth. He coined the phrase, "placing Our Lady's messages as a *'template'* over every circumstance of life." Likewise, with *Mejanomics*, Our Lady's messages are placed as a template over the whole issue of economics to see what Our Lady says about our situation. As he has done with many subject concerning circumstances of life, a Friend of Medjugorje has prayed through Our Lady's messages from the viewpoint of economics to discover what Our Lady wants to reveal to us about today's economic system.

Mejanomics airs every Thursday a live broadcast on **Medjugorje.com** at 12:00 p.m. CST on **RadioWAVE**™. It has gathered a large audience, even from around the world. The book <u>It Ain't Gonna Happen</u>™ was birthed through *Mejanomics* through A Friend of Medjugorje's unique insights into Our Lady's messages in light of today's financial situation.

All past *Mejanomics* shows are available free as downloads. You can obtain them by going online on **Medjugorje.com**, and scrolling down to the bottom of the menu until you see "Downloads". Then click on "Audio" and all past **RadioWAVE**™ shows come up. Or you can sign up for a $10.00 a month donation in which every month you will receive the four shows on CD that had aired that month.

Call **205-672-2000 Ext 315** 24 hours
or Write **Caritas of Birmingham
100 Our Lady Queen of Peace Drive
Sterrett, AL 35147**

If you liked the book <u>It Ain't Gonna Happen</u>™, you will want to listen in on the *Mejanomics* broadcasts, either online or through the mail, to continue learning insights in what you can do to better position yourself for the future when the dollar and the economic system, as we know it, will go away.

Volume Pricing to Get the Word Out
for
It Ain't Gonna Happen

IT AIN'T GONNA HAPPEN!™
A Return to Truth

BF108

(Check One)

☐ 1 $15.00

☐ 10 $70.00 $7.00EA

☐ 50 $165.00 $3.30EA

☐ 100 $280.00 $2.80EA

☐ 500* $500.00 $1.00EA

☐ 1000* $950.00   95¢EA

*Contact for shipping on 500 or more books.

Shipping & Handling

Order Sub-total	U.S. Mail (Standard)	UPS (Faster)
$0-$10.00	$5.00	$9.00
$10.01-$20.00	$7.50	$11.50
$20.01-$50.00	$10.00	$14.00
$50.01-$100.00	$15.00	$19.00
Over $100.00	15% of total	18% of total

For overnight delivery, call for pricing.
***International (Surface):
Double above shipping Cost.
Call for faster International delivery.

ORDER NOW on **mej.com** click on mejmart
or Call **205-672-2000 Ext 315** 24 hours
or Write **Caritas of Birmingham**
100 Our Lady Queen of Peace Drive
Sterrett, AL 35147

After August 1, 2010 order on **mej.com, amazon.com,**
Barnes and Noble, **Books-a-Million** and
bookstores everywhere.

Disclaimer

The subject matter contained in this book is based on Biblical principles and designed to give you accurate and authoritative information with regard to the subject matter covered. It is provided with the understanding that neither the author nor the publisher is engaged to render legal, accounting, or other professional advice. Since your situation is fact-dependent, you may wish to additionally seek the services of an appropriately licensed legal, accounting, real estate, or investment professional.

Limit of Liability/Disclaimer of Warranty: While the publisher and author have used their best efforts in preparing this book, they make no representations or warranties with respect to the accuracy or completeness of the contents of this book and specifically disclaim any implied warranties of merchantability or fitness for a particular purpose. No warranty may be created or extended by sales representatives or written sales materials. The advice and strategies contained herein may not be suitable for your situation. You should consult with a professional where appropriate. Neither the publisher nor author shall be liable for any loss of profit or any other commercial damages, including but not limited to special, incidental, consequential, or other damages.

The author, publisher, and distributor is not affiliated with the United States government, endorse or sponsor the material contained in this publication, nor does the United States government sponsor or endorse the material offered in this publication.

Glossary of Terms

- <u>Ain't</u> — A colloquialism meaning 'is not,' 'are not,' 'am not,' 'has not,' or 'have not.' Though some consider its usage improper, the word is a perennial issue in the English language widely used by many people. It is a profoundly cultural word, used especially in the Southern United States.

- <u>Apparition</u> — Refers to the appearance of the Virgin Mary to different visionaries: to Juan Diego in Guadalupe, St. Catherine at Rue du Bac in Paris, France, St. Bernadette in Lourdes, Lucia, Jacinta, and Francisco in Fatima, Portugal, and now to the 6 visionaries of Medjugorje. According to the Medjugorje visionaries, the Virgin Mary appears to them in a glorified body, in three dimensions. During the apparitions, the visionaries speak to the Virgin Mary, pray with Her, have touched Her, and some have even received a kiss from Her. See mej. com for more information on the apparitions of Medjugorje.

- <u>Apparition Mountain</u> — A mountain located in Medjugorje, Bosnia-Hercegovina, where the Virgin Mary first appeared to 6 children on June 24, 1981.

It is a place of pilgrimage for millions. See mej.com for more information.

- <u>Bullion</u> — Bullion refers to any precious metal in a form in which its primary value comes from the worth of the metal itself (i.e. not jewelry, as its value is partly derived from its artistic/decorative merits), and not from an artificial currency value. Bullion is typically in the form of bars or ingots. The definition can also include coins held as bullion depending upon the use and intent of the word.

- <u>Caritas of Birmingham</u> — Caritas of Birmingham is a mission with international reach that is dedicated to living and spreading the messages of Our Lady of Medjugorje. Founded in 1986, Caritas of Birmingham regularly sends out materials to more than 120 countries across the world.

- <u>Cohesiveness</u> — Sticking together tightly.

- <u>Community of Caritas</u> — The Community of Caritas is a group of people functioning as "one mind and one heart" to operate the mission of Caritas of Birmingham. The formation of the community came at the direct request of Our Lady of Medjugorje when She gave a message to the community's founder,

A Friend of Medjugorje, through visionary Marija Lunetti in 1988.

- Compensation — To be equivalent in value or effect to; to counterbalance; to make amends for.

- Conductivity — The quality or power of conducting or transmitting.

- Consumerism — The promotion of the consumer's interests; the theory that an increasing consumption of goods is economically desirable. In Her monthly message of March 25, 1996, Our Lady of Medjugorje identifies consumerism as a spirit in a negative way of darkness.

- Cross Mountain or Mt. Križevac — A mountain located in Medjugorje, Bosnia-Hercegovina. The villagers of Medjugorje constructed a large cross on the top of this mountain in 1933 in honor of the 1900th anniversary of Jesus' death on the Cross. The Virgin Mary called and continues to call the visionaries, villagers, and all pilgrims of Medjugorje to pray on this mountain.

- Debtor — One who owes a debt.

- Derivative Hedge — A derivative is a financial instrument that derives its value from another asset.

To hedge an investment means to take a financial position to reduce the risk of adverse price movements in an asset. A derivative hedge, thereby, involves using derivative financial instruments to reduce the risk of loss in one's assets due to adverse movements in price.

- Divorce — The dissolution of the marriage contract by decree of civil authority. Though a couple may be divorced in the civil sector, the decree of divorce from a civil authority does not destroy the sacramental union created when a couple is validly married. Jesus states in Scripture, *"I say to you, whoever divorces his wife, unless the marriage is unlawful, and marries another commits adultery."* Divorce is a scourge; a most deadly abnormality; the deforming of the family; the murder of hearts. Read "Who's Opinion is Right, The Painful Truth," by a Friend of Medjugorje for more information.

- Dogma — A doctrine or body of doctrines concerning faith or morals formally stated and authoritatively proclaimed by a church.

- Ductility — Capability of being drawn out into wire or thread; capability of being fashioned into a new form.

- Efficacy — The power to produce an effect.

- Entitlement Mentality — The mentality that a person is "owed" something by society or government because of race, gender, or real or perceived historical suffering. Usually results in chaos to society and the disappearance of morality in law.

- Fatima — A village in Portugal where the Virgin Mary appeared to 3 children, Lucia, Francisco, and Jacinta, over a period of 7 months in 1917, entrusting to them messages for the world and 3 secrets that were to be revealed to the world. The third secret of Fatima was finally revealed by Pope John Paul II in 2000.

- Federal Reserve — The central banking system of the United States. Also called 'The Fed.' Though it is referred to as a government agency, the Federal Reserve is privately owned and is responsible for the issuance of paper currency known as Federal Reserve Notes.

- Federal Reserve Note — A bank note issued by the Federal Reserve. All U.S. paper dollars today are Federal Reserve Notes, and since 1968 are no longer backed by silver. See also 'Fiat Money.'

- Fiat — A term meaning "Let be done."

- <u>Fiat Money</u> — Money, as paper currency, not convertible into coin of equivalent value. Also, money backed by nothing. See also "money."

- <u>Hyperinflation</u> — Inflation growing at a very high rate in a very short time, often considered to be out of control.

- <u>Infill Zone</u> — A term used in Sustainable Development meaning tightly grouped housing areas where people are packed tightly together and have every aspect of their lives controlled. See also Sustainable Development and Smart Growth.

- <u>Inflation</u> — The tax assessed upon the people for the loss of value on fiat money, characterized by an increase in the volume of money and credit relative to available goods resulting in a substantial and continuing rise in the general price level. See also hyperinflation.

- <u>Ingot</u> — A mass of metal cast into a convenient shape for storage or transportation to be later processed.

- <u>Intrinsic Value</u> — The inherent worth of something. Intrinsic value is value that is not dependent upon anything else. For example, silver has an intrinsic value because it has value as a metal that is useful in many applications, as well as exchange for goods and services historically.

- Ivan (pronounced ee-vahn) — Ivan Dragičević is one of 6 individuals chosen by the Virgin Mary in Medjugorje to receive apparitions and messages. As of the writing of this book, Ivan is one of the three visionaries still having apparitions of the Virgin Mary each day. See mej.com for more information.

- Ivanka (pronounced ee-vahn-ka) — Ivanka Ivankovic is one of the 6 individuals chosen by the Virgin Mary in Medjugorje to receive apparitions and messages. As of the writing of this book, Ivanka is one of the three visionaries no longer have apparitions of the Virgin Mary on a daily basis. Ivanka sees Our Lady once a year on June 25, the anniversary of the apparitions. See mej.com for more information.

- Laws of Nature (or Nature's Laws) — Are laws God made which apply to Creation; laws that are characterized by a rule of action dictated by a Superior Being. For example, laws of gravity cannot be changed. Vegetation and animal life are governed by the same laws and they must follow these laws involuntarily to exist. See also "Laws of Nature." The book <u>Look What Happened While You Were Sleeping</u>™ provides an excellent explanation of the differences between Natural Law, the Laws of Nature, and God's revealed law in light of the understanding and intent of America's Founding Fathers.

- <u>Locution</u> — Interiorly and spiritually hearing the voice of Our Lady in one's heart while in prayer; not a physical manifestation.

- <u>Malleability</u> — Capability of being extended or shaped by beating with a hammer or by the pressure of rollers.

- <u>Mammon</u> — Material wealth or possessions, especially as having a debasing influence.

- <u>Marija</u> (pronounced same as Maria) — Marija Lunetti is one of 6 individuals chosen by the Virgin Mary in Medjugorje to receive apparitions and messages. Every 25th of the month Marija relays those messages to the world. As of the writing of this book, Marija is one of the three visionaries still having apparitions of the Virgin Mary each day. See mej.com for more information.

- <u>Mass</u> — The liturgy of the Eucharist; the central act of worship in the Catholic Church. Our Lady of Medjugorje has given several messages about the Mass, encouraging people to not only attend Mass, but to live the Mass, and make it the center of their spiritual lives. See mej.com to search Our Lady's messages about the Mass.

- <u>Master</u> — One having authority over another: ruler, governor; one that conquers or masters: victor, superior.

- <u>Materialism</u> — A preoccupation with or stress upon material rather than intellectual or spiritual things; a doctrine that the only or the highest values or objectives lie in material well being and in the furtherance of material progress.

- <u>Medjugorje</u> — A village in Bosnia-Hercegovina where the Virgin Mary began to appear on June 24, 1981, calling Herself the "Queen of Peace." See mej.com for more official information.

- <u>Mejanomics</u> — The placing of the messages of Our Lady of Medjugorje as a "template" over issues of economics, finances, debt, and common everyday issues, to be interpreted with guidance for a Biblical worldview through the messages of Our Lady of Medjugorje. See mej.com for more information.

- Metric Ton (Tonne) — A Metric Ton is a measurement of weight commonly used to measure precious metals. One Metric Ton is equal to 32,150.75 Troy ounces, or 1,000,000 grams (g). See conversion table on page 293 for additional precious metal measurements and conversions.

- Miraculous Medal — The Virgin Mary appeared to St. Catherine Laboure in France in 1830, showed her the Miraculous Medal, and told her to have a medal struck according to that model. Many people began to experience miracles from the medal, and so numerous and sensational were the cures and miracles that six million medals were made in Paris in the first four years alone.

- Miraculous Medal Medjugorje Round — A silver round designed with images of Medjugorje and sites of Our Lady with information to learn more about Medjugorje on both the front and the back, together with the Miraculous Medal minted upon it.

- Money — A medium of exchange; a means of payment, as officially coined or stamped meal currency.

- Natural Law — Natural law is law that man declares in submission to the laws of nature and of nature's God (laws of nature's God refers to God's revealed law in Scripture). Laws of nature and God's law revealed in Scripture are superior to natural law because they are declared by God Himself. See also "Laws of Nature." The book Look What Happened While You Were Sleeping™, pp. 186–190, provides an excellent explanation of the differences between Natural Law, the Laws of Nature, and God's revealed law in light of the understanding and intent of America's Founding Fathers.

- Our Lady — The term "Our Lady" is a term of endearment and fondness, referring to the Virgin Mary, Mother of Christ. This writing refers to words She has spoken through the worldwide occurring apparitions to six visionaries in a village called Medjugorje. The apparitions have foretold many things about the future, including three chastisements or purifications which will affect the whole world, soon to come to the earth. More is explained on pages iii-iv at the beginning of this book. It is recommended to read these pages, "Story in Brief," to grasp more fully all that is written in It Ain't Gonna Happen™. Go to Mej.com and click on the Ten Secrets in the menu.

- Periodic Table — A tabular display of the chemical elements listed in order of atomic number. As of March 2010, there are 118 elements in the periodic table. Common examples of elements would be: silver, gold, carbon, oxygen, iron, uranium, helium, etc.

- Prayer Group — The term "Prayer Group" refers to a prayer group formed by Marija, Ivan, and others at the request of the Virgin Mary in Medjugorje. Our Lady asked them to assemble on Monday and Friday nights on Apparition Mountain or Cross Mountain. At certain times the group gathered on Tuesday, but they regularly meet on Monday and Friday.

- Production — Production refers to mine production, the quantity of a precious metal that is brought above ground from underground mines.

- Providential — Of, relating to, or determined by Providence; occurring by or as if by an intervention of Providence.

- Reprobate — Morally abandoned, depraved; foreordained to damnation.

- Resumption of the Cult — To reinstitute a following to a devotion.

- <u>Rosary</u> — The word rosary means "garland of roses." The rosary is a circular string of beads used to offer a set of prayers to God through the Virgin Mary and Her intercession. Praying the rosary is central to Our Lady's call in Medjugorje, and She has given the rosary a new efficacy in these times.

- <u>Scapular</u> — A pair of small cloth squares joined by shoulder tapes and worn under the clothing on the chest and the back as a sacramental. There are many different types of scapulars in existence today. The scapular referred to in this book is the "Brown Scapular" given to St. Simon Stock in 1251.

- <u>Silver Certificate</u> — A type of money printed in the United States between 1878 to 1964. Silver Certificates used to be redeemable for the same face value in silver dollar coins. An act of Congress removed the obligation to back silver certificates with silver bullion starting on June 24, 1968.

- <u>Silver Eagle</u> — An American investment grade silver bullion coin, made of pure .999 fine silver. The coin was authorized by Congress in 1985 and first minted in 1986.

- <u>Smart Growth</u> — One of two main arms of the global land use component of Sustainable Development.

It is the plan to control every aspect of individuals' lives (housing, water, wells, energy, employment, etc.) once they have been forced into "infill zones." Smart Growth uses land condemnation or special zoning plans to alter privately owned property in order to create these infill zones. Read the book <u>Look What Happened While You Were Sleeping</u>_{TM} to gain a more complete understanding of Smart Growth and its role in Sustainable Development. Download the audio book or book on mej.com

- <u>Sustainable Development</u> — A plan for global control having 3 components: 1. **global land use,** 2. **global education**, and 3. **global population control and reduction**. Sustainable Development is a euphemism, a seemingly innocent name given to something sinister in order to hide the truth. Read the book <u>Look What Happened While You Were Sleeping</u>_{TM} to gain a more complete understanding of Sustainable Development.

- <u>Tilma</u> — A poncho-like cloak made of cactus fiber. The image of Our Lady was miraculously imprinted on Juan Diego's Tilma after he filled it full of roses to show to the local Bishop in obedience to Our Lady's request during one of Her apparitions to Juan Diego. Because the Tilma was organic, it should have deteriorated within 3 years, yet the Tilma and the image are still intact today, five centuries after the apparitions.

- Toxicology — A science that deals with poisons and their effect and with the problems involved.

- Troy Ounce — A Troy Ounce is a measurement of weight most commonly used to measure precious metals. One Troy ounce is equal to 1.0971 ounces, or 31.103 grams (g). See conversion table on page 293 for additional precious metal measurements and conversions.

- Usury — The lending of money with an interest charge for its use. St. Thomas Aquinas wrote:

"He commits an injustice who sells wine or wheat and who asks for double payment, i.e., one, the return of the thing in equal measure, the other the price of the use, which is called usury.... Now money, according to the Philosopher [i.e., Aristotle], was invented chiefly for the purpose of exchange; and consequently the chief and principal purpose of money is its consumption or alienation whereby it is sunk in exchange. Hence it is by its very nature unlawful to take payment for the use of money lent, which payment is known as

usury: and just as a man is bound to restore other ill-gotten goods, so is he obliged to restore the money which he has taken in usury."

Scripture Verses for Strength and Discernment:

1. Exodus 22:25 *"If you lend money to my people, to the poor among you, you shall not deal with them as a creditor; you shall not exact interest from them."*

2. Deuteronmy 23:19 *"You shall not charge interest on loans to another Israelite, interest on money, interest on provisions, interest on anything that is lent."*

3. Psalm. 15:1, 5 *"O LORD, who may abide in your tent? Who may dwell on your holy hill? ... (those) who do not lend money at interest, and do not take a bribe against the innocent."*

4. Luke 6:34 *"If you lend to those from whom you hope to receive, what credit is that to you? Even sinners lend to sinners, to receive as much again."*

5. Leviticus 25:36–37 *"Take no interest from him or increase, but fear your God; that your brother may live beside you. You shall not lend him your money at interest, nor give him your food for profit."*

6. Proverbs 28:8 *"He who augments his wealth by interest and increase gathers it for him who is kind to the poor."*

7. Jeremiah 15:10 *"Woe is me, my mother, that you bore me, a man of strife and contention to the whole land! I have not lent, nor have I borrowed, yet all of them curse me."*

8. Ezekiel 18:8 *"Does not lend at interest or take any increase, withholds his hand from iniquity, executes true justice between man and man."*

9. Ezekiel 18:13 *"Lends at interest, and takes increase; shall he then live? He shall not live. He has done all these abominable things; he shall surely die; his blood shall be upon himself."*

10. Ezekiel 18:17 *"Withholds his hand from iniquity, takes no interest or increase, observes my ordinances, and walks in my statues; he shall not die for his father's iniquity, he shall surely live."*

11. Ezekiel 22:12 *"In you men take bribes to shed blood; you take interest and increase and make gain of your neighbors by extortion; and you have forgotten me, says the Lord God."*

12. Matt 6:19–21. *"Do not lay up for yourselves treasures on earth, where moth and rust consume and where thieves break in and steal, but lay up for yourselves treasures in Heaven, where neither moth nor rust consumes and where thieves do not break in and steal."*

A Small List of Common Uses of Silver

coinage
bullion bars
photographic emulsions
photographic paper
rings
earrings
watches
religious medals
silverware
hollowware
electroplating
table settings
batteries
bearings
GPS systems
antennas
brazing
solder
catalysts
computer chips
cell phones
switches
relays
electrical controllers

hard drives
flash drives
compact discs
radios
microphones
wireless mics
medical tools
medicine
sanitation
disinfectant
burn cream
cloud seeding
dental fillings
mirrors
coatings
platings
tinting
solar panels
water purification
washing machines
clothes lining
radiography
microfilm
aircraft engines

turbines	medallions
railroad engines	chalices
missiles	ciboriums
torpedos	monstrances
spacecraft	inks
bombs	patens
calculators	inverters
cameras	tabernacles
hearing aids	automobiles
circuit breakers	aircrafts
motor brushes	laptops
slip rings	smoke detectors
timers	DVD's
thermostats	tanks
speakers	cables
headphones	audio connectors
printers	wall plugs
mixers	LCD Screens
ipods	x-ray machines
wireless cards	generators
clocks	foil
motors	deodorant
pumps	bells
inverters	makeup
paints	pendants
light bulbs	dye

Common Units Used for Precious Metals and Their Conversions

1 Troy Ounce = 1.0971428571 ounces

1 Troy Ounce = 31.103 grams (g)

1 Metric Ton = 32,150.746 Troy ounces

1 Metric Ton = 1,000,000 grams (g)

Recommended Reading and Other Sources to Further Your Education

Below is a list of books and websites that will help you deepen your understanding of what is covered in this book in regard to the economic substance as well as the spiritual and other related topics that may not appear to be economic in nature on the surface.

Look What Happened While You Were Sleeping $_{TM}$, by A Friend of Medjugorje

The Creature From Jekyll Island: A Second Look at the Federal Reserve, by G. Edward Griffin

Aftershock, by Wiedemer, Wiedemer, Spitzer

Hurtling Towards Oblivion, by Dr. Swinson

Tipping Point, by Malcom Gladwell

www.usgs.gov, United States Geological Survey

www.silverinstitute.org, The Silver Institute

www.mej.com, Source on Medjugorje and the apparitions of Our Lady of Medjugorje

Mejanomics Radio Programs, hosted by A Friend of Medjugorje, visit mej.com

<u>Words From Heaven</u>®, by A Friend of Medjugorje—most comprehensive book on the messages of Our Lady of Medjugorje.

INDEX

Endnotes

CHAPTER ONE

1. http://www.olrl.org/sacramental/rosary.shtml
2. "Why did the 'Unknown Light' Predicted by Our Lady at Fatima Appear Precisely on January 25, 1938?", Jim Condit Jr., http://www.realnews247.com/rakovsky-interrogation.htm

CHAPTER FIVE

3. *"Preuves et Documents sur l'Apparition de Marie à Alphonse Ratisbonne 20 janvier 1842"* — by René Laurentin
4. Compiled from information taken from http://seanhyland.wordpress.com/2009/01/21/503, review of source documents including the transcript of Claude Newman's trial, and interviews with Br. Claude Lane, OSB, who has performed extensive research on the Claude Newman story.
5. Transcript of Fr. Robert O'Leary's personal involvement with Claude Newman.
6. Ibid.
7. Vicksburg Evening Herald, May 19, 1944
8. Ibid.
9. http://seanhyland.wordpress.com/2009/01/21/503
10. Ibid.
11. Vicksburg Evening Post, February 4, 1944
12. Transcript of the Court Record of Claude Newman's Official Sentence.
13. Transcript of Fr. Robert O'Leary's personal involvement with Claude Newman.

CHAPTER SIX

14. Notebooks 1945–1950, by Maria Valtorta, pp. 564–565
15. God Alone, The Collected Writings of St. Louis Marie de Montfort, Montfort Publications, pgs. 302–307

CHAPTER SEVEN

16. *Who's Opinion is Right, The Painful Truth*, by a Friend of Medjugorje, p. 22
17. *"Five Tips For Couples Considering Divorce During Economic Slump"*; http://www.cadivorce.com/divorce-tips/5-tips-for-couples-considering-divorce-during-economic-slump
18. *"Divorce Rates Drops Due to Bad Economy,"* FOX News, December 23, 2008
19. How To Change Your Husband, by a Friend of Medjugorje

CHAPTER EIGHT

20. "Delaying Kids May Prevent Financial 'Motherhood Penalty'", http://www.usatoday.com/money/perfi/2010-04-15-Having-kids-early-economic-penalty15_ST_N.htm?csp=34&utm_source=feedburner&utm_medium=feed&utm_campaign=Feed:+UsatodaycomHealth-TopStories+(News+-+Health+-

+Top+Stories)
21. Money and Wealth in the New Millennium, by Norm Franz , 2001, White Stone Press, page 154

CHAPTER NINE

22. Tipping Point, Malcom Gladwell
23. Information from several formal interviews conducted with Andrija by A Friend of Medjugorje
24. Look What Happened While You Were Sleeping™, by A Friend of Medjugorje, p. 217
25. http://findquotations.com/quote/by/Joseph_Stalin
26. Look What Happened While You Were Sleeping™, by A Friend of Medjugorje, p. 213
27. http://www.gold-eagle.com/editorials_02/mbutler021502pv.html

CHAPTER TEN

28. The Visions of the Children, Janice Connell, p. 82

CHAPTER ELEVEN

29. http://www.measuringworth.org/datasets/gold/result.php and http://goldinfo.net/silver600.html
30. http://www.goldprice.org/spot-gold.html
31. U.S. Geological Survey, Mineral Commodity Summaries, January 2010, Silver and Gold
32. "An Overview of Gold's Supply & Demand", by James Turk, http://www.kitco.com/ind/Turk/turk_feb252008.html
33. http://www.invest.gold.org/sites/en/why_gold/demand_and_supply/
34. Avg. of calculations up to 2004 from http://www.gold-eagle.com/editorials_05/zurbuchen011506.html, plus yearly mine production data from USGS, Mineral Commodities Summaries, 2006 through 2010
35. http://silverstockreport.com/2008/out.html
36. World Silver Survey 2009
37. Ibid.
38. U.S. Geological Survey, Silver Mineral Commodity Summaries, January 2010
39. Ibid.
40. http://silverstockreport.com/2008/out.html Hommel 14–16
41. "Why Silver, Why Now?", Monex Metals
42. Ibid.

CHAPTER TWELVE

43. http://www.sterling-silver.ws/articles/about-silver/medicinal-uses-of-silver.htm
44. http://www.silverinstitute.org/medical_applications.php
45. http://www.scienceline.org/2008/04/18/tech-heger-silver/
46. http://www.silverinstitute.org/medical_applications.php
47. http://www.annieappleseedproject.org/fournatanag.html

48. http://www.silverinstitute.org/medical_applications.php
49. Monex Metals

CHAPTER THIRTEEN

50. Right Side News, "Five More Years of Hard Times" Note: Partial fiat currency systems have lasted longer than 50 years, but full fiat paper currencies have not lasted for more than 50 years.
51. http://www.ustreas.gov/education/faq/currency/sales.shtml
52. http://oll.libertyfund.org/?option=com_staticxt&staticfile=show.php%3Ftitle=807&chapter=88161&layout=html&Itemid=27
53. Abraham Lincoln, November 1864, *History Through Quotations*, wichaar.com
54. Recovering the Lost Art of Common Sense, G.K. Chesterton

CHAPTER FOURTEEN

55. Financial Peace Revisited, by David Ramsey, pg. 10-11
56. The Creature from Jekyll Island, by G. Edward Griffin
57. Ibid.
58. Ibid.
59. Ibid.
60. www.vatican.va
61. http://www.sspx.org/catholic_faqs_morality.htm#usuryasin
62. Ibid.
63. Ibid.
64. Ibid.
65. Ibid.
66. Ibid.
67. Ibid.
68. The Creature from Jekyll Island, by G. Edward Griffin
69. freddiemac.com/pmms/pmms30.htm
70. http://oll.libertyfund.org/?option=com_staticxt&staticfile=show.php%3Ftitle=807&chapter=88161&layout=html&Itemid=27

CHAPTER FIFTEEN

71. World Silver Survey 2009
72. "Why Silver, Why Now?", Montex Metals
73. http://news.silverseek.com/SilverSeek/1273257866.php
74. http://www.invest.gold.org/sites/en/why_gold/demand_and_supply/
75. http://www.coinnews.net/2010/04/01/american-silver-eagle-coins-rally-in-march-capping-u-s-mint-quarterly-sales-record/
76. Calculated using annual US mine production from U.S. Geological Survey, Mineral Commodity Summaries, January 2010
77. http://www.silverinstitute.org/medical_applications.php

CHAPTER SIXTEEN

78. Catherine Laboure: Visionary of the Miraculous Medal, Rene Laurentin, pg. 275

79. Webster's New Collegiate Dictionary
80. Ibid.
81. <u>Catherine Laboure: Visionary of the Miraculous Medal,</u> Rene Laurentin, pg. 96
82. Obtained from the Congregation of Our Lady of Zion.

CHAPTER EIGHTEEN

83. <u>God Alone,</u> The Collected Writings of St. Louis Marie de Montfort, Montfort Publications, pgs. 302–307
84. Ibid.
85. "Revealed: The true horror of everyday life in Zimbabwe," by Mark Tran, <u>www.guardian.co.uk</u>
86. *"The New Economy of Hunger,"* Washington Post, April 27, 2008

CHAPTER NINETEEN

87. <u>Catherine Laboure: Visionary of the Miraculous Medal,</u> Rene Laurentin, pg. 53
88. Ibid., p. 120
89. Ibid., p. 120
90. Ibid. p. 120
91. Ibid., p. 120
92. Ibid., p. 121
93. Ibid., p. 159
94. Ibid., p. 187
95. Ibid., p. 187
96. Ibid., p. 211
97. Ibid., pp. 176–177
98. Ibid., p. 177
99. Ibid., p. 172
100. Ibid,, p. 169
101. Ibid., p. 169
102. Ibid., p. 118
103. Ibid., p. 115
104. Ibid., p. 115
105. Ibid., p. 115–116
106. Ibid., p. 115–116
107. Ibid., p. 118
108. Ibid., p. 208–209
109. Transcript of Fr. Robert O'Leary's personal involvement wth Claude Newman.
110. <u>Catherine Laboure: Visionary of the Miraculous Medal,</u> Rene Laurentin, p. 115–116